AF478702

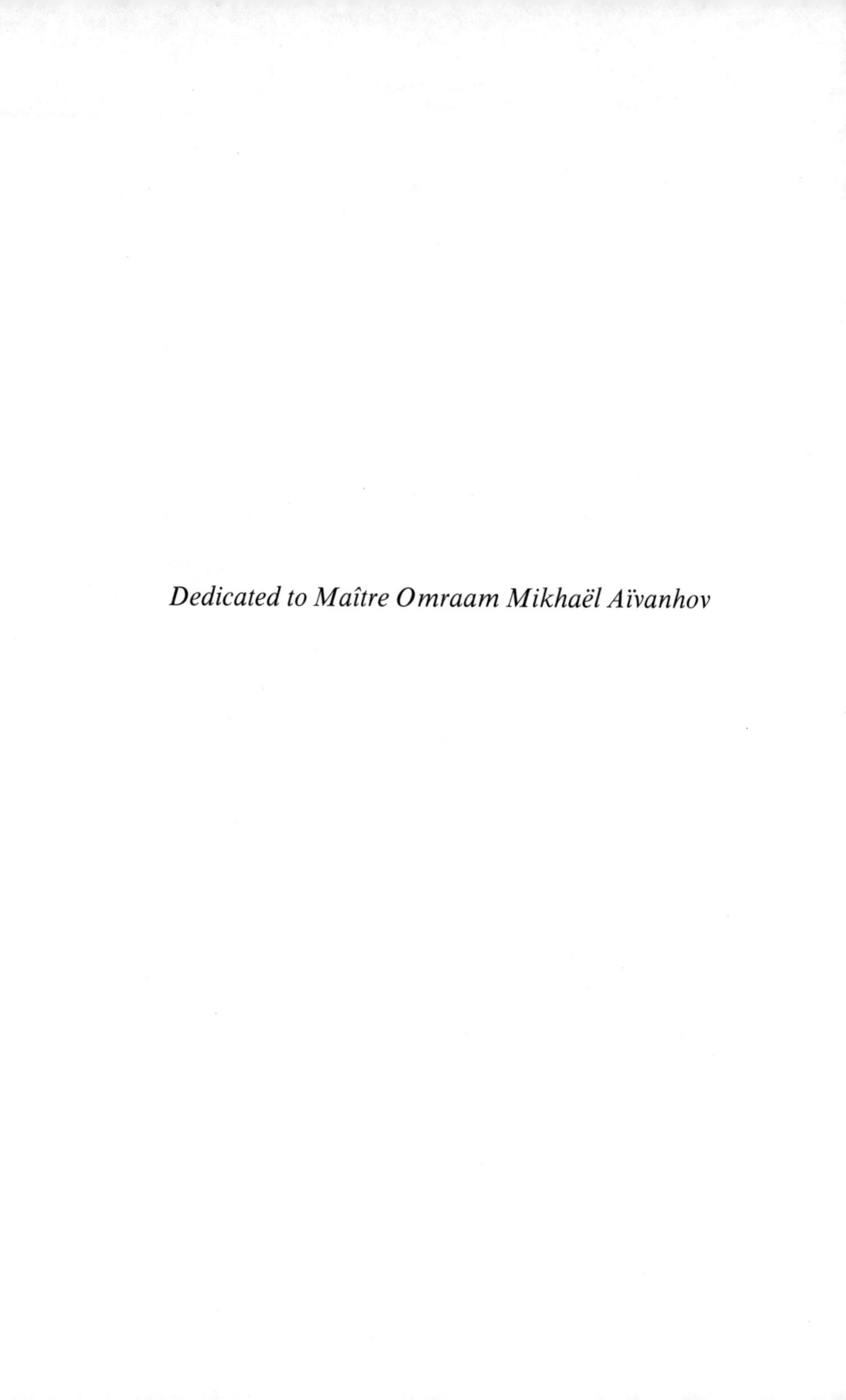

*Dedicated to Maître Omraam Mikhaël Aïvanhov*

# THE SOLAR REVOLUTION AND

# THE PROPHET

## *The Role of the Sun in the Spiritual Life*

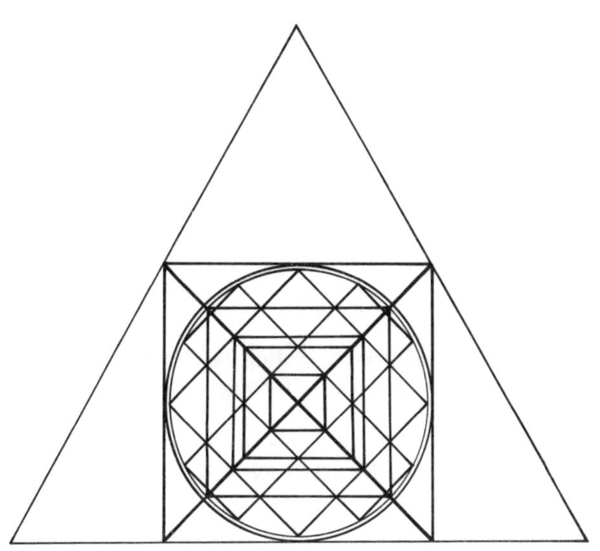

Pierre C. RENARD

PROSVETA EDITIONS

CONTENTS

FOREWORD : The statement of a Disciple ......... 9

I  THE EXAMPLE ................................ 11

II  THE SUN, Historical Image of Joy ................ 17

III  THE SOLAR SEER ........................... 33

IV  THE INITIATIC AND ESOTERIC SCHOOL OF
MAÎTRE OMRAAM MIKHAËL AÏVANHOV

**First, the Heart:** The Solar Revolution
or the New Romanticism of Aquarius ............. 63

**Secondly, the Form:** The Brotherhood
that Took the Sun for Model ..................... 77

- The World of Light ............................ 86
- The World of Love (warmth) ..................... 94
- The World of Life ........................... 106

**Thirdly, the Meaning:** The Way to Brotherhood ... 121

- A Master Evolves... Toward Perfection .......... 123

- Evolution Toward Perfection :
The Way of Hope ........................... 126

- Evolution Toward Perfection :
The Way of Power ......................... 128

- Evolution Toward Perfection :
The Only Way to Solve
the Problem of Survival
in a Brotherly Way ........................ 131

- Evolution Toward Perfection :
The Way to Joy ........................ 144

- Evolution Toward Perfection :
The Authority
or a World Government ...................... 152

- Evolution Toward Perfection :
Spiritual Alchemy* ........................ 160

EPILOGUE : For the Time of the Prophet Approaches .. 173

- The Cosmic Hierarchy ........................ 175
- The Golden Age ........................ 181

Omraam Mikhaël Aïvanhov

# FOREWORD

## *The Statement of a Disciple*

In France, Maître Omraam Mikhaël Aïvanhov, an Initiate and the most extraordinary Being of our time, has been, for nearly forty years, donating a new Teaching to the world: an ideal, a culture, of Brotherhood for all men, founded on the Sun!

Not only does he give us the means and methods of the new culture, but he is himself the example of the new type. Because this constitutes an event in itself, terribly important for the world and for mankind, I have made it the subject of this book... the statement of a disciple.

The Teaching of the Maître comes at this particular moment in the history of civilization, when the vernal point passes into Aquarius (a scientific event that inevitably changes civilizations whenever it occurs) which will involve the whole world in a solar revolution. It is the signal for the coming of Brotherhood for all peoples, of the Initiates, and of the Golden Age. Whether we believe this or not is immaterial. It is a Cosmic event, consisting of currents of force far beyond the control of man, whose choice is either to submit, or to participate.

Maître Omraam Mikhaël Aïvanhov says :

«All the necessary elements are now present for the Kingdom of God to come on earth. The only obstacle is unwillingness on the part of humans, who refuse to give up their old concepts and change their habits, who refuse to accept or participate in the work, but go on taking care only of their personal affairs. Under these conditions, the Kingdom of God will never be realized; should the world consent, it could come very quickly. The important thing is consent. If we were to accept the ideas of a great Initiate, the Kingdom of God, the Golden Age, would be here immediately. But it must be a real Master that wins the consent of mankind, with knowledge based on the laws of life and how to live, and not only on external facts... chemistry, physics, mechanics, etc...

A fabulous future lies ahead for the youth of the world. I call the awakening of our consciousness the New Romanticism of Aquarius, engendered by the solar revolution which has already begun.

The term solar revolution is not to be taken in the astrological sense, i.e. the revolving of the Sun back to a certain degree in time, which occurs once a year. Solar revolution is used here in the sense of the occurrence of events, changes, and upheavals, as the vernal point enters a new Sign or Constellation of the Zodiac (a sign and a constellation being two different things).

The Sun, as it enters the Constellation Aquarius, will stir up and release certain events known only to the Initiates.

As to the meaning of the word evolution, the reader is asked to have in mind a movement toward perfection of form and content and principles as envisaged by Cosmic Intelligence, not evolution as Darwin, Lamarck, or Ernst Haeckel understood the word.

Pierre C.RENARD
Spring 1978,Ville d'Avray

# CHAPTER I

# *THE EXAMPLE*

To-day, as the world moves into the 1980's, we have no illusions when we wake up in the morning concerning the presence of brotherhood in the world. Things are not easy. No illusions either concerning our politics and our leaders and the power they wield. They may use the word brotherhood because they have to, they have no choice, but their thoughts are elsewhere, busy with economics. Take the problem of oil, for instance. To enhance their own value, the oil-producing countries raise the price of oil, whereupon the consumer-countries react, make adjustments, and economize... the result being that there is no profit for the producers, necessitating another price rise, etc. etc... This is called speculation. It is a way of life: ours. Do you see any future for brotherhood there? Brotherhood is non-existent, simply because our political leaders never think about it. No need to look further than that for the reason.

Others, however, think about nothing else: the Initiates. In the Great Universal White Brotherhood, they've thought about it for centuries. Again and again they tell us that it is all they think about. They prove it, they sacrifice themselves for it. And to-day (the great news) they announce the coming of

Brotherhood, it will be here before the end of the century. They are prepared for it, the Initiates. And since they have never been wrong throughout all history, we must believe them.

A little old lady, pale and pinched, paused at the stand, her eye caught by the words on the cover of a book: «Before the End of The Century, The Golden Age Will Be Established on Earth Under the Leadership of The Initiates.» She glanced at us sideways. It was at the Book Fair, in the spring of 1978, amid the dust of the old Bastille station. She tried to smile ironically, but it was more of a simper. «There are good Initiates and there are bad Initiates», she declared (don't be taken in) and glided off in her pallor, pinching the air as she went. We are familiar with this refrain, it is our daily bread whenever we mention the word «Initiate». For thousands of years I have listened to it! Are there good Initiates and bad Initiates? I don't know. I don't care. I know what I know, which is that ever since I met one, thirty years ago, my life has been marvellously transformed. He had the goodness to accept me as a disciple when I was not even hoping for it. And to tell the truth, he never asked me whether I was good or bad.

It is this great living Initiate, Maître Omraam Mikhaël Aïvanhov, whom I will try to describe for you. To begin at the beginning, when I am asked about this Master, who and what he is, I answer: «He is a perfect example, a live model.» And I have said all that needs be said. I have testified. And I have justified myself, for if I choose to follow this Master, it is because of what he gives me without ever asking a thing in return... the example, the model... himself! Weigh those words with care. If I follow him, it is not for the protection of his aura, not with the fanatical devotion of a Pharisee, not in order to sit on the right hand of God, not even to save my soul. Certainly not for the opportunity to ply him with compliments and flattery; even if I tried, as some do, I would be unable, I am too awkward. Neither is it for the extraordinary knowledge and genius of this Master (reason enough, God knows); no, it is because of something else that is very rare: example. His example. Knowledge is taught in all the auditoriums of the world, but it has never produced... brotherhood. And as for examples! This example patterns himself on the Sun, that is his example.


Did you know that example is the only thing that really affects us, that lasts? The only thing. Of all the people we meet in our lives, the one we remember best is the one who strikes us as an example, who impresses us with the qualities he exemplifies. In love, it is our concept of love (the model, the pattern) that fills us with joy. Example warms our hearts and stays with us, because it reveals us to ourselves: that is the power of example.

The first thing a child does, the first gesture hc makes, is to imitate what he sees and then do it himself (becoming a model) to show others how strong he is. The need for a pattern is written in our genes that we may see ourselves... it is our heritage, our antiquity, our continuity, our human eternity, our secret psychic motive. The youth of to-day lacks a high example, that is the trouble; and they let us know it, they don't hide it!

Therefore, when we meet a Being who has taken the Sun for model, whose life is patterned on the Sun, how can you keep from crying out: «Brother! Neighbour! I have found the most extraordinary person!» A Being who has taken the miraculous, the marvellous, as the model to live by, as an example, and who makes that kind of living available to us too, by making it come alive in front of us. The example. The Brotherhood of the Sun! He makes us see our own suns. That is the extraordinary, marvellous thing happening to-day unbeknownst to scientists or philosophers or political leaders, because that is not what they think about, their thoughts are elsewhere.

I remained with this Master, and what did I learn? To wake up in the morning in time to watch the Sun rise, to give thanks for the life the Sun gives to us. Thousands of us are here doing the same thing each morning, on the hill at Sèvres, or in summer on Mount Esterel, or in Greece, Canada, Belgium, England, Germany, Switzerland, Israel, Africa, Italy, Japan, India... wherever the solar disciples of Maître Omraam Mikhaël Aïvanhov meet, at dawn, to follow the example of the Initiate, our model.

The Sun an example! Unusual, to say the least; impossible to talk about without a shiver of delight. Who is the model of all the people one sees on city streets? Who is the model of all the people one thinks of as exemplary, whose morals and manners, language and policies we copy (at the moment)... who is their model? How can one believe in the brotherliness of some one speaking on television who has not a trace of kindness in his face? How can one believe in the serenity of this disciple of Gurdgieff who chain-smokes while he speaks to you? Who is their model? If I have faith in brotherhood, it is only because of this Master who is the very model of brotherhood. He makes us have faith in ourselves, that is the magic! Do you realize how unusual that is, to-day, when people waste those things... energy, health, faith, brotherhood, man himself? It is a moving experience to discover how much it takes to be an example, and what an example! A solar example! Try it and see how much control you must have over your thoughts, feelings, and actions. And also over circumstances. Control over the imponderables, the emanations and radiations, the auras, the subtilities. Control over the «contingency».

CHAPTER II


# *THE SUN*
## *HISTORICAL IMAGE OF JOY**

** Author's note: History relates the facts of man's evolution and the humanities. But it is evolution itself that is memorable, rather than facts, which are fragile, disputable, forgeable, precisely because they are an account, a record. Whereas evolution is an incorruptible force. Here, historic means whatever concerns the evolution of man and humanity: the solar force that makes history!*

Once you decide to follow a Being who has taken the Sun as his model, your ideas are bound to change. There is a cleansing of the heart... with celestial water. You are no longer the same, you are better, you feel better. No one can lead you round by the nose any more. When I watch our learned scientists, philosophers and political leaders on television, searching for truth while scratching their heads ponderously, I cannot help thinking they are wasting their time: truth is already discovered! It is, and always has been, there, in the Sun! If the truth, theirs, yours and mine, is to be alive, really and entirely alive and intact on all planes, then there is no doubt about it, that is where truth is, in the Sun. The Sun is the source of all life, the source of everything that lives. No use scratching one's head! No use, no use at all.

The Sun is the source of life. Forgive us, Father, we forget that; we are thinking of other things. And yet, the Sun is there! All day long, in our wheat fields, in our vineyards and orchards, up to the moment night falls. Sun for the bread and the wine. Sun aplenty! Come and see for yourself, my brother. We did, we climbed the hill and there it was, behind the Being whose model it is. We relive a great childlike joy when we see the Sun, and recognize it. Day by day, to the rhythm of light, we hear again the ancient song of life. Things that we had forgotten. We learn how to embrace the Universe and plunge into its immensity (we were taught, we learned, we practised, my brother). So, look, if one day you meet him, this Being who has taken the Sun as his model, shut your eyes and follow him blindly: you will see everything more clearly. No longer will you waken to oil crises and monetary depression, but to the heartbeat of this example of Light. That is the difference. You will rediscover a taste for transparency, for clear springs, for gratitude, for the rhythm of light, with no recompense other than this daily joy. You will discover yourself in your soul, in the fullness of your heart. And you will no longer be able to do without, the rest recedes into the shadows. You will do your utmost and go far beyond your ability, because you know the simple truth: everything comes from the Sun.

No biologist will be the one to contradict this, they are the first to believe that everything comes from the Sun including our life, our flesh and our blood, in spirit and in truth. The Sun is the pattern, the master pattern for everything alive, for all creations, his creations... that is the surprise... the truth that touches us to the quick. Colour, fragrance, flowers... the Sun is the unique source! The «return to the source» that people talk about is the return to the Sun. When there is talk on television about extra-terrestrial beings, when we make films about creatures from other planets, when we imagine encounters with a third species, we know that it is really human beings who are the extra-terrestrials, we are the people from another planet, the Sun, and our species is solar. People don't say these things because they are not concerned with a solar example, they have other things on their minds. And as people listen, as we listen, we woolgather, we think about anything but the idea of a solar model. Thus, at our expense is history made.

For without that idea, our heart is cut off from the source of life, it has no way of knowing about grandeur, power, and glory. That we didn't know, we hadn't thought about that. We think we know that our bodies and hearts have identical needs, that everything in us is related, that we can be brought back to life and restored to health by a beautiful day or a great love: we've experienced the relationship between our hearts and bodies millions of times. We think we know all this, but actually we don't know it, since when we expose our bodies to the Sun, we leave our hearts behind in the shadows, the shadows of our misery. And as neither scientists nor philosophers told us differently... our heart is now cut off from the source of life. That is the trouble, Mr.President, our heart is thirsty for the Sun. Dying of thirst! The proof: the more we try to force our heart to drink from some other source, the more we ply it with pleasure and security, the thirstier it gets. That is the modern paradox. The more we accentuate pleasure and safety, the more anguish and anxiety we feel. Psychologists' offices are filled to overflowing with the sickness of thirsty hearts. Our chronic anxiety. I don't mean difficulty and hardship, which has always been the salt of the earth and the stimulus of history... survival has never been easy... not in the time of dinosaurs, not in the time of Jesus on the Cross, not in the time of genius, knighthood and cathedrals... And it is not easy now, as this age draws to an end. I mean anguish: when you no longer enjoy life, when you lose the joy of living. When nothing is wonderful any more and there is no hope. Nothing but emptiness. Without the Sun. Frustration. That is when violence rushes in, it invades the streets and nothing can stop it, no prohibition, no organization, no law. What ignorance! Violence is there at the end of each neuron, and has been since the beginning of history, in us. A thousand billion bazookas in a thousand billion cells, and as many atomic submarines in the depths of our subconscious. There, normally and naturally, to protect us. To insure our animal survival on earth. Violence plays its part well, no complaints. One must only be aware of it, there in the warm pit of our stomach, prepared for its historic role, which is to insure the continuation of history, to strengthen our instincts so that we will know how to procreate, eat, digest, breathe and suck milk from the breast in the first few minutes. In the roots. The trouble is, it shouldn't come up out of the earth, it shouldn't overflow out of the belly into the heart, that's all. When it invades the heart with its bazookas and atomic devices, man goes to pieces. His cells become frightened, his nervous reserves are soon exhausted, his brain clouds over, his solar plexus closes up, his endocrine glands secrete poison, all his organs become asphyxiated, his skin exudes nauseous gases, the circuits are blocked. Panic! The viscera contract in spasm, the belly empties itself, and the face turns pale, all because anguish invaded the heart! It is a clinical fact. Depression. Coronary thrombosis. War. Now, to-day. Because the Sun abandoned our hearts. Because we no longer think about the idea of a solar model.

Yes, that is the truth as it was given to me by a Being who takes the Sun for model. The Sun, image of our happiness! This is not folklore and fairy tales, it is the historic message of survival. In order to understand in depth, we have to understand where we live... not only on our street, but in a Universe of forces with the Sun in the centre. It is these great lines of Cosmic force that make us live and cause us to survive, transpiercing us, animating us and assuming charge over us. We are merely condensers, capacitors, coming from the Sun, thus proving that our heart needs a solar model in order to survive! It's that simple. When I say heart, I don't mean the muscular heart which is already a solar model in imitation of the Sun; nor the abdominal heart, the solar plexus which has the role of reservoir, vital and solar; I mean the sentient, susceptible, responsive heart that makes the man of heart, the virtuous heart, the wise, loving, active heart. The consciousness of ourselves in our inmost secret depths. The soul, come from Heaven. A spiritual (not material) reality within, formed by each instant we live, by our sensitivity, our thinking. In brief, the imaginative heart. The heart that distinguishes us from the rest of the evolving species by its power to create images. Our cosmic role is to create images! We need do no more than that, create images, for our inner life to survive, even though we don't realize it. Children have picture books, we reward them with pictures, we love to look at pictures, television fascinates us with pictures, and we all have a picture, a certain image of ourselves, of our success. In short, our image is our inner reality. That is why our souls need a model! Our imagining puts us in rapport with the Cosmic forces that go through us;* as they come from the Sun, they bear the Sun with them: the model they offer our imagination is nothing but the Sun! You see how simple it is, how true historically? Nothing new. For millions of years our cells have been little solar mirrors,** and our heart a solar memory.*** Our

---

* Cosmic forces become crystallized in minerals, become movement in vegetation, become sensitization in animals, and imagination in man. See «Before the End of the Century» by the author.

** the nuclides.

*** The word heart designates the centre of a system, i.e. the physical heart in the circulatory system, the solar plexus in the neuro-vegetative system, the Hara Centre for the auric system, the liver for the digestive system; all centres, or hearts. Also the neocortex (the brain's grey matter), as yet unexplored, which supports our sensitive consciousness in its position behind the brow, and seems to be the centre for association, integration, a synthesis of all sensorial messages and hence of the image. This is our human privilege. As for solar memory, it is invariably in the solar plexus. The superior-

reality is imaginal, our imagery is the Sun! All the PSI powers
are there! Which is marvellous since we all love the Sun.

And look at the way the world is organized: each thing in
its place, each thing essential to the whole. Three lines of
Cosmic force emanate from the Sun, corresponding exactly to
our secret idea of happiness, three solar virtues called light,
warmth, and life (a trinity!); the light of knowledge for our
minds, the warmth of love for our hearts, the power of life for
our bodies. What more do we need? Money? We will have it
if we have the power of life inside. Happiness? Not unless
there is warmth and love in our hearts. Intelligence? Not if
your brain is clouded over. And which do you prefer, to be
drab, cold and deadening, or full of light, warmth, and life-
giving qualities? Can you imagine love without the Sun? Or a
future without light, warmth, and life? The point is made, is
it not? The idea of happiness we make for ourselves is the
same idea the Sun has. Without that idea in our hearts, violence takes over... and there we are... no use reaching for
tranquilisers. This is so basic, so elementary and so obviously
true that one wonders why our learned philosophers and
world leaders (who should be models for our hearts to live
by... it is their role) spend so much time thinking of other
things. That is certainly not what they tell us... are they afraid
of what people will say? Don't they know that they inspire us
with boredom and a distaste for life? That they are paving the
way for violence, that they are themselves violent? Don't they
know that we are part of a Universe which grants us the forces
we summon with our imaginations, according to the model
we choose to imitate?* If, one day, man is powerless to stop

______________

ity of an Initiate lies in knowing how to decode the image (see «Before the
End of the Century», by the author).

* For the corresponding Sephiroth according to the Kabbala, see «The
Mysteries of Iesod» and «The Splendours of Tipheret», Volumes VII and X
of Complete Works, Maître Omraam Mikhaël Aïvanhov.

the currents of violence he has released in the subconscious, it will be because of the Cosmic forces that penetrated our hearts, because of the model we patterned our lives on. They say that in 1979, the cost to the country will be 5,000,000 Francs **per minute** for the production of armaments (against violence). I have trouble understanding this; it makes me afraid.

And then there are those who refuse to be taken in, who don't obey conventions or follow the example of contemporary leaders. Those who are alive in history, proving that they never cut themselves off from the source of life, they never allowed for the suicide of the heart; those who were, and are, a light for man to go by. In short, those who were obviously initiated in the Sun, and who took the Sun for model.

Those whom we call the Initiates.

What are Initiates? Mages? Magicians? Sorcerers? Prophets? Messiahs? Imposters? We don't know. We get everything mixed up. We believe and at the same time we don't believe, like that, without ever being sure. And if they had never existed? How convenient that would be! So much is said about them, so much folklore. They are made to appear divine, which is something they never asked for; neither did they ask for people to kill each other in their name. They are thought of as belonging to India when actually they have been more often in France over the last two thousand years. Also, and this is more frequent, they are apt to be in constant danger of their lives, pursued, beaten, burned, crucified, submitted to inquisitions from the press, to the ignorance and ridicule of people, to the stupidity of sects,* as they were two thousand years ago in the time of Jesus, or some two thousand years before that, in the time of Moses. It all depends on history.

We learn as part of our catechisms that there are Beings of a higher order and a higher dimension, who shared the same high ideal and finished with a higher form of death (Jesus, Zoroaster, Krishna, Orpheus, Pythagoras, Hermes, Ram, Buddha, etc.) once they had stated the truth. That we know. But what truth were they talking about? We don't know any more. What was the truth they all spoke, these higher Beings, that made them die a higher form of death? A truth unbearable to the existing order, to the scholars, the philosophers, the leaders, that caused them to die on the Cross at three o'clock, or burn to death at the stake, or be pierced by the sword... in any case, drained of their lifeblood? Those are the Beings who brought truth to light (initium = initiate), but what truth? What truth concerning the origin of things could be so unbearable to the existing order, if not the truth that the Sun is the beginning, the origin of all living things, the perfect model? Unbearable, that truth, for all the other models, the scholars, philosophers, and political geniuses who thought of themselves as the instigators of all things. One has to become humble and kneel before the truth. Before the Sun! Unbearable! And so they built crosses, heated the irons, released the wild beasts. Here is where history becomes unforgettable. Even with their blood pouring out they refused the accepted order, the earthbound, material worlds, geocentric, egocentric, claustrophobic worlds where great white birds die on beaches blackened with oil. They foresaw the Hell of those worlds, it is their word. They didn't give in. They filled their

---

* Author's note: The initiators of sects are never Initiates: an Initiate, as we shall see, does not create sects. His Teaching is universal, not sectarian, he is a solar magus. All parties are sects.

hearts with Sun. They followed the Sun's example. And what was meant to happen, happened. They blossomed! Flowered! They accelerated their evolution. Evolution, which is the universal principle of survival, leading all things to their flowering, to grandeur, power, infinity... and immortality. They obtained what they wanted: self-mastery. As a result, they became our Masters and our superiors in the Cosmic hierarchy. The never-to-be-forgotten great Beings of history. With complete control over themselves and over the forces of Nature, over all circumstances. A control derived from some other means, other organs that they developed and that we don't even know about. They became Suns. With total power, total competence and strength, total greatness; with a philosophy, a science of life, a knowledge of the future. With a divine policy, an idea for a world government already formed, waiting for the day when it would assume the destiny of the world.* Treating us with kindness, as an older brother would his junior. Describing repeatedly, since the beginning, the forces that emanate from the Sun and rebound from the stars and constellations, making the planets evolve and revolve the earth as an ocean wave rolls a shell. With us inside, outside, above, below: man living in his solar milieu.

None of this is recent, no one knows when it began. The beginning? Perhaps ten thousand years ago on the banks of Titicaca in Tiahuanaco, the golden city of the Sun, modeled on the Sun, at the time when the vernal point passed into the Constellation of Leo, where the Sun is master. Or more recently, when Ram fled Europe and the druidesses of the Moon, taking his solar civilization with him to India, where he developed the Vedic culture he bequeathed to mankind. Then Krishna took up the relay, and imitated the Sun. Still

* See «Before the End of the Century» by the same author.

later came the great solar civilizations along the Mediterranean, in Chaldea, Assyria. And Zoroaster in Persia also took the Sun as his model. When the vernal point passed into Taurus about six thousand years ago, the solar civilization was in Egypt, in the Pyramids where the great came from far and wide to be initiated by Hermes: Moses and Jesus from Judea; Pythagoras, Orpheus, and Plato from Greece.

All, including their disciples, took the Sun as their model. Going back to the beginning of things, studying man and the Universe, gave them the answer to the three fundamental questions: how to survive, how to love, and how to live together. In short, how to be happy.*

They put the answers in their sciences, Magic, Alchemy, the Kabbala, Astrology (Ah! the forbidden sciences), four sciences that gave birth to our materialistic sciences, Physics, Chemistry, Mathematics, Astronomy, all concerned with the object: the form and power of the object (Physics), the study of its constituents (Chemistry), its proportions (Mathematics), and its position in space (Astronomy). Initiatic science is concerned with man and his solar milieu. Yes. Apply the same definitions to man and his relationship with the Sun, and you will have, in the same order, Magic, Alchemy, the Kabbala, and Astrology. Are they ridiculed by the learned, the philosophers and the political leaders? So much the worse for them. No one has the intellectual prowess or the command of facts with which to deny these four essential sciences, their origin is too remote, it goes back further than history. They are the sciences of the «beginning», the sciences of Initia-

---

* Three aspects of happiness corresponding to the three basic instincts in each living cell, each living organism, each living creature: self-conservation (survival), self-reproduction (love and sexuality), self-government (living according to law). See drawing in Chapter IV.

tion.* There is nothing weird about them, on the contrary. They enlighten man by means of the Sun, source of life. They indicate to us our chances for survival, happy survival! They link our hearts with the Heart of things. The Sephirotic ladder shows us the link that exists between our imagination and our organs, between our organs and the different regions of the Universe and the beings that belong to these different regions. It's extraordinary, isn't it? And completely comprehensible for us, our organs were formed originally by this solar Universe! Everything is bound together, in spirit and in flesh, by the visible and the invisible, by what is above and what is below, and by all that is sacred. Those are the true human sciences to which we are now gradually returning... the long way round.

The Initiates revealed progressively their inspired plan for the survival of mankind, according to the epoch in which they lived, according to the Constellation then influencing civilization, and according to the development and capacity of men's hearts and brains at that particular time. This explains why the knowledge of the beginning was veiled for those who couldn't understand, but available and clear for all who opened their hearts. For instance, to indicate the process of entropy** which rules the Universe (the two forces circulating in our cells, the current of life and the current of death, evolution and involution) the Initiates invented the idea of good and evil, so that man would learn to swim in the Cosmic

* Author's note: Modern encyclopedias place these sciences of the beginning... at the end! The definition of the word encyclopedia: «A work that treats comprehensively all the various branches of knowledge in the interests of a complete education.»

** Principle of the degradation of energy: everything that is born must die. Signifying that life is forever renewed.

ocean and save his life by heeding the warning: if he allowed his heart to become caught in the current of death, the current of fear and contraction, he would lose everything.

To prove the need for this polarization of the two forces, the Initiates created the symbol of the Cross, and told us about night and day, light and shadow, Heaven and Hell, the Sun and the earth, Spirit and matter, Adam and Eve. To stir the imagination of men and make them aware that it is just this opposition of the two Cosmic forces that permits him to survive, to symbolize the four elements through which Cosmic polarity manifests itself, and to gather all these things under one heading, the Initiates created the Name of God. To explain the Universe to man, the central Source that summarises and explains it all: God, the Beginning and the End.* When you explain to children about fire, before you allow them to handle it, you tell them a little at a time. For thousands and thousands of years, during solar revolution after solar revolution, the Initiates became progressively clearer, less and less veiled as they described the different ideas pertinent to each era of the civilizations they launched, Gemini, Taurus, Aries, Pisces. They introduced ideas into the mind and understanding of men that conformed with the influences of each sign, the signs also having been determined by the Initiates. For instance, we still have an interest in stone, we like to go back into the past in search of our spirituality, now lost in the bog of materialism. If everything Hindu has become fashionable in the West (are we trying to justify our frozen hearts?) could it be because Hatha-Yoga means «link with the solar electromagnetic forces»? What was good for the past is no longer good to-day, the planets must revolve and complete their solar revolutions: Aquarius is rising on the hori-

* God is the symbol of the Genesis of the World, revealing the anatomy, the physiology, and the psychology of the world. See Complete Works, Maître Omraam Mikhaël Aïvanhov.

zon of history. We must rethink, recreate, a new conception of things, of life, not by the abolition of the senses, nor by the complete passivity of an egoistical and uncommunicative Nirvana, like the spiritualists. Nor by the abstraction of the materialists who overlook the fact that man is alive. Since those things existed, they were no doubt necessary, but I believe they no longer correspond with the needs of man. Man needs the Sun. He needs to eat fire and drink the light! That is the **solar revolution** now beginning. Just as the **industrial revolution** led to today's **scientific revolution** (to obtain an improvement in the quality of life), so that revolution leads to a **solar and spiritual revolution.*** It will begin, many think, with the advent of Aquarius, the powerful current of fire and light that will introduce a new man to the world, the solar man. Next will appear an Initiate, to set the example for the solar man to follow. A magus, from the Sun.

* Author's note: The astonishing thing is the acceleration of this movement of profound and progressive transformation of the social, economic and moral order, as we approach the end of the century, the cosmic expiration of term. The agricultural revolution took its time and moved to the rhythm of the wheel barrow. From the rural economy of the villages, which Charlemagne attempted to change, through long centuries of feudal economy in the hands of the landowners, through the commercial explosion resulting from research, discovery, and the invention of banking systems, to today's industrialization of hens' eggs and overfed calves, took 1,000 years. The industrial revolution was briefer: it started in the 16th century with the steam engine, the mechanical weaving machine, and burst out triumphantly with electricity, gas, trains, and all kinds of technical ability, in the 19th century. One might have thought that the Golden Age had arrived and that we would be able to breathe at last! Some visionaries were romantic enough to believe it. They forgot that life is for the living, for the acceleration of evolution, and that the scientific revolution was already upon us: chemistry, biology, medical research, the microscope, the telescope. In the 18th century, there were academies, now there is data processing, and science is moving toward the quality of life. Quality is something spiritual, a need of the heart. Certain consciousnesses are already participating in the solar and spiritual revolution, which will occur before the end of the present century. The result will be the new man, living in a new social order.

# CHAPTER III

# *THE SOLAR SEER*

Has it ever happened to you to run into a magus on the street? Consciously? Do you ever dream about those legendary heroes who knew how to bewitch people and things at will? Imagine that one grey morning you leave for work as usual, walking calmly. You come to a crossing. The red light changes and you cross. Someone passes you. You hardly notice, you are preoccupied with your thoughts. But suddenly, yes, you feel something magic happening: you are bewitched! The street is full of light, the air vibrates strangely, you see rainbows! You turn around: too late, he has vanished. But you... Oh! Wonder of wonders! You feel completely rejuvenated, liberated and detached. Your brain is filled with some higher intelligence, clearer and brighter than before; your heart beats faster and more easily; life circulates warmly in your arteries, stirring your will and filling you with power. You have been transpierced, heart and soul, by a ray of Sun. A celebration! If this ever happened to you, wouldn't you do everything to find him again, this mysterious magic Being? Suppose you did find him, wouldn't you want to follow him, listen to him, live near him through the years, watching, observing, learning, while the extraordinary Being goes on indefatigably illuminating consciousnesses, warming hearts, stirring will powers? Until it gradually becomes clear to you that he thinks of nothing but the Sun, the Sun is his model, the model for his life, and he makes every effort to emanate the same virtues, the same light, the same vivifying warmth, the same power, the same pervasive gentleness, the same rigour and implacability. The same indestructibility. And everywhere, the trinity that you begin to think about all the time: light, warmth, life. Well, that is what I lived when I met Maître Omraam Mikhaël Aïvanhov. I assure you my life was transformed, illuminated, warmed and revived by the trinity of light, warmth and life that now gives it meaning. The solar trinity that emanates from the Initiate. Not only in his words, not only in the radiance of his auric presence, like a ray of Sun, but specially in the example he sets, the image he presents that penetrates our sky and stirs our imagination (with light, warmth, and life) even without ever meeting him, like that, simply by closing the eyes. I close my eyes, I think about this Master, I consider the Initiate: it is a privilege. I immerse myself in the consciousness of this extraordinary person, whom I know to be absolute truth, absolute incorruptibility. Like an oasis. Forgotten, the aridity of the path across the desert that led to him... I try to sense who he is, and I discern him best among those who launched man and humanity. And even if I was not sensing him correctly, I had only to open my eyes and watch him live, watch the example he gives; white is white, how can I explain it any other way? It is the statement of a disciple. For more than thirty-five years he has appeared to me like his predecessors in history, exactly as I imagined them with awe when I first read about them. Was it they who taught him, or was he their Teacher? How can one tell? These dimensions are beyond us. But I know what I saw. I saw this Being live as a solar model.

The Sun acts on the earth's elements to bring them to their flowering; in the same way, the power of a Master acts on the elements of our inner life. Our cells are not lifeless, and once enlightened, warmed, enlivened, they dance the dance of the electrons and set in motion, in their nuclides, the secret code of evolution, perfection and flowering, the joy of survival! In our hearts, a thousand billion cells exploding a thousand billion times with the solar code! How could one not feel better? We have met the magician, the Magus, the enchanter, the one that lightens our consciousness, sets our hearts on fire, and spurs our wills (thus Jesus raised the dead). Light to lighten our days and take away our distress, warmth to make us love one another, and life, naturally, for our health! Whatever else I hear seems pale beside the great simplicity of the Initiatic message: light, warmth and life. The three needs, all we need, for each instant! Light, warmth and life. The solar power of the Initiates! Magic!

Magic? A simple word, entirely clear. A familiar word. An everyday word. Yes, we perform magic all the time, every day. All of us. We either help or hinder our selves, do we not? That is magic, no more than that. We influence the state of our soul, our day, our friends, for good or for evil. So and so either attracts us or makes us uncomfortable, such and such a thought has a good or bad effect on us. That is our power: to be able to influence our aura, our atmosphere, our neighbours, our collective environment. No need to look further. There is magic in our looks, our gestures, our habits and obsessions, our speech, our secret thoughts, in everything around us, the colours, forms, concrete, flowers, grey sky or blue... everything affects us, either for good or for bad. And in order to survive, we affect everything else. Magic is the power of survival! Most of us perform black magic, meaning that we use our power to satisfy ourselves. We apply it to objects, a role in life, a friend, a brotherhood, a Master, always with the goal of satisfying our needs. Initiates are white magicians, solar magicians! They use their power to help mankind. They use it in the enthusiasm of their generous natures so far as to sacrifice themselves, so far as to face death on the Cross above Golgotha, if necessary. They give themselves as the Sun does, demonstrating the power of example. The power of the beginning. Initial, Initiatic power. The original PSI (the word to-day) power, the weapon of the declining century. One imagines staffs of methodical sorcerers of the sixth sense, organizations of black magicians with headquarters all over the world, parapsychologists plying their techniques. I say to them that the Initiates have surpassed them for thousands of years, and will go on surpassing them for another thousand years as far as light is concerned... fortunately for the world!

The Initiates of all time (and to-day) have understood that the original power – solar – was inscribed in our cells once and for all, obligatorily, in the memory of our nuclides. It's up to us to discover that power. They left us the means to do so, with the root: «mag». A message, a code to decipher! It was doubtless traced first of all in Sanskrit* and then transferred from one culture to another. If you are at all curious, you will find that this «mag» belongs to all the world's languages, always signifying power. The power of action. «I can!» Magia, in Bulgarian; Machen, in German; Make and Magic, in English; Mage in French; Magus in Latin; Mago in Greek derived from the Persian, which derives from the

* Author's note: probably the oldest known language, Sanskrit is Indo-European, the classic language of the Brahman civilization in India. Was it the first Initiatic language? All we know is that the earliest record of Sanskrit known to mankind, is the VEDAS (= knowledge), the Initiatic texts inspired by the teaching of Ram. Sanskrit (= perfect) was the language in use for thousands of years before our era. According to Maître Omraam Mikhaël Aïvanhov, there existed another Initiatic language prior to Sanskrit which is never mentioned, there are no records. It was called: Vatan.

Sanskrit. In short, the important thing is for your heart to know that it has magic power. It can!

It can do wonderful things. Rouse your curiosity enough to look in the dictionary! You will notice that all the words signifying grandeur, splendour, power, contain the root «mag». Magnus! The magnificent root! Magnificence! Magnanimity! Magnetism! Majesty! Notice that imagination, your imagination, comprises the same historic root. In ancient times, the «imago» was the Magus. The image is our inner power: in-mage! And the quality that distinguishes man is, as we have seen, the ability to imagine. He is the creator of images in the Cosmos, it is what places him above the animals in the Hierarchy, and paves the way for him to reach out for the new currents of force that will carry him to Heaven. He intensifies his power, as one forces the growth of a plant. He becomes powerful. Do you see what a solar magus is? Someone who has taken the Sun as his model and uses the resulting power to increase his creative imagination, control it, and restore it to its solar role, radiation! Restoring light, warmth, and life, and imagining solar hereafters! If you think this is easy, try it! You will see what it means to be an Initiate. You will understand the Master I am trying to describe. You will understand his power. You will understand that the Masters are the ones who are responsible for all of mankind's great spurts of creativity in the Arts, Sciences, and Civilizations.

People who still think of the Sun as a mere ball of fire (who created the ball of fire?) must know that the Initiates considered the physical Sun a proof of the existence of a spiritual Sun, an omnipotent Cosmic Spirit, in the same way that our creations prove the existence of our spirit.* It is not the

* Author's note: Maître Omraam Mikhaël Aïvanhov explains the words of

hand that does the creating, but the spirit behind the hand. We live in a Universe where everything visible is the reflection of an invisible force, where matter is the condensation of either spirit or energy. Throughout history we find this revelation of the Cosmic Spirit animating matter in different ways, depending on the era and the place. It was Agni, for the Vedic peoples; it was Osiris, for the Egyptians. «Aleohim!» exclaimed Moses, when the Angel of the Lord appeared to him as a flame in the heart of a bush on Mount Sinaï. It was love in the heart of Jesus: «Our Father Who art in Heaven...». Princeton scientists are now referring to the Father as Cosmic Consciousness. The same Power, the Solar Spirit, whom the Initiates call Christ. Christ, a reality perhaps, but too far off in a Heaven too high above. Most of us don't believe any more, we are resigned, we are what we are. Others dream mystic dreams. Christe Eleison! For the Initiates it seems clear. It is the supreme Power, the supreme Light that lightens the darkness, the invisible, supreme Warmth that actuates the spheres, the supreme Life that ressuscitates eternally (no one knows when it began and who can predict the end?) Spiritual light, spiritual warmth, spiritual life! The peak of the PSI power we talk about: Christ. Absolute puissance, of which the Sun is the image and likeness: light, warmth, life! I believe this is the way to think about the things that give us life here on earth, the way that satisfies our mind, our heart and our will to survive.

------

the Psalm: «I will walk before the Lord in the land of the living...». «The land of the living,» says the Master, «is the Sun, the home of noble and luminous beings whose light shines so strongly through their emanations and vibrations and radiations, that it also shines on us. The light that shines on the planets does not come from the Sun, but from the inhabitants of the Sun... the Sun is a fertile and cultivated land, a whole civilization, inhabited by Initiates who project their light on us. Our scientists will discover this one day. Initiates have long known how to visit other planets and the Sun in their etheric bodies, they travel everywhere in space. This is the truth... you can believe it or not, as you like.»

For the Initiates, Christ is a state of consciousness. They live this state of consciousness, they talk it. They are called Jesus-Christ, Moses-Christ, Buddha-Christ. They make it clear that there was a historic being who lived and played his part called Jesus, who in his consciousness, was the Christ. In his solar evolution, he was Christ, Christlike, living in a state of Christhood. A soul beyond our understanding, with room in his soul for several solar systems. Vertiginous! This would explain the extraordinary lives of these Beings, their extraordinary power. The sublimity of their lives. Perhaps the peak, the highest intensity of life ever to exist in our system.

Maître Omraam Mikhaël Aïvanhov revealed to us once that there had been eighteen Beings in all to arrive at this state of sublime consciousness, eighteen among all the rest, who are the greatest, the most important Beings ever to have lived. He added that the nineteenth was being prepared by Providence and would soon appear... I am overwhelmed, not so much by the fact that there are nineteen of them, but that this Master could tell it to us with such authority and power... it's this power that makes me think, or rather dream...


To give you an idea of the extraordinary scope and capacity of this Master, I will tell you some of the astonishing things that happen in his presence, or in his name. I will do this, dear reader, so that you will have a complete picture of the Initiate, knowing that these few incidents among so many (it would take several volumes to cite them all) will surprise and puzzle you. The really surprising and unusual thing is that this Being has never admitted to being responsible for what happened, always answering that it was not he, but «others» who take care of those things, and that if there were good results, well, it was by chance! Adding (can I even write it?) that the scientist Jacques Monod, the Nobel Prize winner, was right... this, when in the past the Master has been terribly critical of this scientist's philosophy, based on «chance», but when the kind of thing I am about to describe happens, he quotes Monod, saying that it happens quite by chance! Modesty? Nevertheless, I believe what I (and my friends) have seen with our own eyes.

Now let us see what Brother R.M. says about a trip in the company of the Master in the Pyrénées: «...in the middle of the narrow road, blocking the way, was a stalled truck; the gear shift was broken and the truck could be moved neither forward nor backward, which meant that we would be blocked for hours. Brother Mikhaël, as he was called prior to his trip to India in 1958, got out of the car, approached the truck, and bent over the gear shift with interest. No one could tell what he was doing, but one thing was certain: he knew nothing whatsoever about motors or trucks or anything mechanical. A few minutes later, he said: «Go ahead, now try it.» The driver was skeptical: «It won't work, I've been trying for an hour. Anyhow, I took the gear shift apart...» «Try it!» repeated Brother Mikhaël gently, persuasively. The driver climbed behind the wheel. Stupefaction! The motor started and the truck moved ahead, just enough to park on the side of the road and let us by!»

This story lived in the memory of the enthusiastic smiling man full of daring and courage called Brother J., our friend. He served the Maître faithfully all his life. He told us many stories about him, all stupefying. Here are three more stories having to do with cars.

«A few years ago, Giani Esposito and the Maître were in Italy. Their trip drew to a close when they heard that they must be back in France on a certain date. As they left Venice, the car began to behave alarmingly, to such an extent that they realized it would be impossible to drive it all the way to Paris (which was essential). The Maître got out and began talking to the stalled car which was belching forth black smoke, saying that it was imperative for them to be at Sèvres at a certain hour, that they were unable to contact a garage because it would take too much time, that the car was to make every effort to get them to Sèvres, where he promised to take care of it and see that all the necessary repairs were made. The Maître patted the car as he talked and then in they climbed. To Giani's great astonishment the car, with a good deal of noise and smoke, not only started but worked perfectly all the way to Sèvres, right up to the front door, whereupon it caught fire. It was completely done for. The garageman couldn't believe that a car in that condition had brought them so far.

«Another time, four of us were at Sèvres to greet the Maître and Giani Esposito as they arrived from Sweden. We escorted the Maître into the house and then went back to open the trunk and take out the suitcases. In vain! Yet they were the right keys... for a long time we tried everything, and finally someone went to tell the Maître. We all watched as the Maître came and stood before the car. Then he addressed it in a tongue none of us understood, apparently commanding it with great force. We were all amazed for he never talked that way to anyone, even when we deserved it. Then, turning to us he said quietly: «Go ahead, turn the key in the trunk.» It opened instantly. The Maître smiled at us; we stood staring at each other.

«And another time, the Maître was about to take the train from Lausanne to Paris, when the car that was to drive him to the station refused to start. There wasn't a minute to spare: the Maître would miss his train. The Maître spoke to the car, asking it to be kind enough to go at least as far as the station. The car started. The funny thing is that it ran for thirty kilometres, it got us to the station, but came to a dead halt in the middle of the street and refused to budge. The Maître made the train, but the car remained where it was, blocking traffic in front of the station until the police came and towed it away!»


I can't give you the exact number of people who have been healed by the Maître, but there are many. One case in particular impressed me, described in the book «Who Is The Maître Omraam Mikhaël Aïvanhov?»

«At the Bonfin, in 1958 (says Brother J.), Dr. Daguzan and I were sitting with the Maître when a man drove in, wanting to discuss with us the sale of his property at Bagnols-en-Forêt. The land was nearby and highly desirable, and the Maître invited him in. His arm was in a sling because of an infected finger, he told us, which refused to heal in spite of all the doctor's prescriptions. Our interest was roused because he was obviously in great pain. He told us that the surgeon wished to operate on the finger and would probably amputate it. Dr. Daguzan questioned him about the infection, during which time the Maître meditated, eyes closed. When the doctor was through, the Maître said:

«You are married, are you not?»

«Yes, Maître.»

«You have two children, have you not?»

«Yes, Maître, a boy and a girl.»

«But before you married their mother, you lived with another girl?»

«Yes, Maître.»

«Did you promise to marry her because you wanted to possess her, and then did you abandon her for someone else?»

The man burst into tears and fell on his knees, clasping the Maître's hand in his.

«Get up, my friend, calm yourself,» said the Maître. «I am not judging you. Nor do I blame you or condemn you. But I want to make you see things as they are.»

The man stood up, unable to stop weeping, overwhelmed by the Maître's insight.

«What should I do, Maître?»

«You must make repairs.»

«How, Maître?»

«By going to see the girl, who has not been able to marry because she has your child. She is ill, the child is ill, all because of the tremendous weight she has to bear. Go as quickly as you can, offer her your help, ask her to forgive you. She is the key to your being cured. Your visit and the financial help you are going to give her will make her well, and the child also. Go and do that, my friend, before the sun goes down. In a few days, your finger will be healed.»

«But Maître, what about the operation, since the finger is already gangrenous?»

Dr. Daguzan spoke up.

«I assure you, Maître, medically speaking, the surgeon is right, the finger is already beginning to stink: it should be amputated.»

«I know, I know,» said the Maître. «But repentance... when we are really sorry and do everything in our power to make amends as soon as possible, can release tremendously powerful, positive, and constructive forces that alter the situation. Believe me, dear brother, and you too, my friend, you must believe me: if you will do as I say, you will be healed.»

The man covered the Maître's hands with kisses and left, his face smeared with tears.

I ran into him a week later in Fréjus. He came up to me, smiling, happy, no bandages on his finger.

«Brother J.,» he said. «Would you please tell the Maître that he was right: I did what he told me and I am cured, completely cured. Thank him for me, thank him, thank him!»

There is apparently a tremendous power in the name Omraam Mikhaël Aïvanhov. I wonder about it. So many of our brothers and sisters have been saved by this Name that is about to take its place in the history of mankind. Here are two more passages from the same book.

«Something very surprising happened recently, in Paris. One of our sisters, R., closely bound to the Maître by her feeling of admiration and respect, was attacked on the street while she was walking home after one of his lectures at Sèvres. Still full of the lofty ideas she had been hearing, she was deep in thought and completely unaware of being followed. Suddenly she found herself on the ground with a man on top of her, in imminent danger of being raped, robbed or rubbed out, who knows... she did the only thing she could think of: with all her strength she cried : «Omraam Mikhaël!» As though hit by some unseen force, the man let go and ran off into the night. Sister R. got to her feet, intact, surprized, amazed. She told us about it herself.

«Another time, in Switzerland, Sister M., a young teacher, was driving her car along a precipice above Sierre, in the Valais. Suddenly, on one of the steep turns, her brakes gave way and the car aimed for the precipice, out of control. With all her heart and soul she cried out: «Omraam Mikhaël! Save me!» The car came to a stop at the edge of the precipice. You can imagine the state of joy and gratitude this sister was in. When she went to thank the Maître for saving her life, he answered with a smile: «It was not I...»

Food for thought.*

---

* Author's note: these revelations will seem strange to anyone who wasn't there, because materialism has deadened our hearts. You have only to turn on your television to see how prejudiced our scientists are. For instance, as an experiment, they take a bowl full of water, put a fish in it, and register the electromagnetic impulses emitted by the fish with a receiver that transforms them into audible vibrations. You can hear the message of survival emanated by the fish! Proof that the fish in the sea have means of telecommunication we don't know about or ordinarily hear. Very good. But do our materialistic scientists admit that telepathy exists between men (who have in addition, a cortex and a brain)? Do they admit that man has an effect on

This summer another young sister told me what had happened to her while hitch-hiking, something that the Maître had asked her not to do. Disobeying, she waited on the road for a car to stop; it was not long before two young boys stopped for her and she got in. At the end of a kilometre or two, they started making odd proposals, suiting the action to the words. She fought them off, but they were determined. Seized with panic, she yelled with all her might: «Omraam Mikhaël!». The boys stopped as if struck by lightning, opened the door, and let her out: a narrow escape.

How often it happens, when you tell the Maître about a situation that appears insoluble, that a day or two later everything falls into place! One day a sister, M. de R., told the Maître about her financial difficulties... if only the person she had lent a large sum of money to years ago would pay her back! But the person was now in America and years had gone by without a word. The Maître comforted her and told her not to worry. She received the exact sum of money from America a few days later.

Now I will tell you what happened in September, 1977, when the Maître was at the Bonfin, near Fréjus, for the summer camp. One day, the brothers and sisters telephoned from Sèvres to tell him what happened: that day at sunrise, a light had appeared in the East and grew larger and larger as it

---

material atoms that are transpierced by currents of electromagnetic forces? When they are confronted with proof, do they admit that it might be more than coincidence? What bothers me is not so much that scientists give men less opportunity than they give to fish in a bowl, but that they want me to believe Nature has come to a full stop... that all evolution ceases with the fifth sense... that that is all there is! I don't believe this. My meeting with the Initiate proved that there exist beings more evolved than we, with higher senses than ours and receivers and emitters that we have not yet developed.

climbed the sky. The brothers and sisters saw it clearly as a flying saucer. What surprised them most was that the flying saucer remained stationary for a quarter of an hour directly above the terrace of the Maître's apartment! A few minutes later it disappeared, and they watched as two helicopters circled and circled overhead, apparently sent by the Astronomic Observatory at Meudon to investigate.

Who knows how close the Maître is to the Angels of the four elements, particularly the Angel of Air? I admit, dear reader, that I am troubled by the things I have witnessed and continue to witness... things that may seem to you like inventions, but I promise you they are real.

Once, just before nightfall, we were all worried because of the frightening nearness of a fire in the woods near the Bonfin. There was not a cloud in the sky and the strong wind blew the fire closer and closer to us. Several of the brothers and sisters went to warn the Maître. Together they climbed to the Rocher (where we watch the Sun rise) to observe the fire. It was only a little distance away, behind the Capitou, and we were directly in line. The Maître asked them to leave him alone. In no time, clouds appeared in the sky, and as the Maître was returning to his chalet, the heavens opened up and a torrential rain fell... extinguishing the fire. The next day, the newspapers were full of praise for the firemen, but there was no mention of rain!

This summer, for three whole months the Maître showed us what a good friend he has in the Angel of Air. For three months, day after day, we had a blue sky, a radiant Sun, never a cloud, until the brothers complained to the Maître about the dryness of the crops. From then on it rained every night, but every morning the whole Brotherhood would be on the Rocher watching the Sun rise! At the end of camp, the 29th of September, the Maître warned us that it would probably rain, for he had thanked the Angel of Air for giving us such perfect weather all summer... with the suggestion that the Angel was now free to do as he liked. The day after the feast of St. Michael, the rain poured down from the sky and continued for days.

One last account by an eye-witness: a magic display of colour. Brother R.M. describes the end of an expedition with the Maître (then Brother Mikhaël) in the Pyrénées.

«The Sun was going down on the horizon and the fog was rising from the valley, signaling the end of the outing, the time to go home, when, as we started down the mountain, there suddenly appeared before us the projection of our silhouettes on the thick screen made by the fog, each silhouette surrounded by its concentric aura. Brother Mikhaël's aura was tremendous, ours seemed very small and insignificant in comparison. Around each of our heads appeared a golden circle that melted into other circles of colour, blue, yellow, and red, and then vanished into the fog. Brother Mikhaël went striding down the mountain ahead of us, cutting a path through the fog, waving it back with commanding gestures, his voice echoing back to us to indicate the way...»

Now, here is another proof: yes, it was given to me to see the permanence of the Solar Spirit in all its antiquity and continuity. In its supreme PSI power. I have absolutely no visionary power, I assure you. There were many of us, a whole crowd. We all had proof that this Master is linked to the Solar Spirit and that he thinks about nothing but following its example. I am not going into all the thousands of details proving that the Master is constantly being assisted by higher entities from the invisible world, but it is a fact that he arrived in France with very little money in his pocket, no knowledge of the language, no friends to turn to, and no visa but the one authorizing his stay during the Universal Exposition of 1937! But things **happened,** a multitude of events around him made it possible for him to settle in France, to be protected, to be helped materially, whether you believe it or not. However hideous the trials he had to undergo subsequently – corruption, lies, profanation (interesting that of all those who slandered him during those thirty-five years, most were punished in some way by the invisible forces, and several have already been dispatched to the other world...) – he always came out of the worst trials nearer than ever to our ideal of a Master.

It is à propos of this sacred image, the ideal that we bear in our hearts like a code, that I will tell you about the event that has already taken its place in history for those who were there. It will serve as an answer to those who claim that a Master is capable of deforming the Teaching of his Master. Idiots! Accusing both Masters in one stroke, one of deviating from the truth, the other of lacking foresight! Impossible, short of penetrating the consciousness of both at the same time. The Christly consciousness! It would require being able to enlighten, warm, and enliven men's hearts. And resuscitate the dead.

It was at Orly, twenty years ago. A marvellous day. We were, several of his disciples, there to greet the Maître Omraam Mikhaël Aïvanhov upon his return from India, where he had met with other Initiates, specially Babadji. We had not seen him for a year. What would he be like now? He was about to arrive... intense emotion... there he is! We catch sight of the shining white silhouette we know that even the crowd seems to respect. He is here. Stupefaction! We are struck dumb, frozen in this moment of history. He is no longer the same! Even his nose is different! There was no doubt about it, he was the image of his Master, Peter Deunov. He looked like what we imagine the world's great Initiates looked like, proving that they all had the same model. The child I held in my arms said: «It's Moses.» It was Moses. And it was Jesus, it was Hermes, it was Ram, it was Omraam Mikhaël Aïvanhov. Reflecting the Sun, his model. This Spirit, this Christ, returning from India with his new name for history, OMRAAM, «He who dispels the darkness». With the triple name, Omraam Mikhaël Aïvanhov, which adds up kabbalistically to something of great Initiatic significance (that I am not free to disclose). Returning for the sake of Brotherhood on earth, here in the world. Foreseen, we repeat, by other Initiates, the clairvoyant founders of great spiritual movements, such as Hanish, Master of Mazdaism; Leadbeater, Master of Theosophy; and Steiner, Master of Anthroposophy... foreseen for some time before the end of the century. Because – they said – the evolution of the world will then enter the era of Mikhaël. Mikhaël, the solar Archangel who, according to tradition, overcomes the dragon... what else but the dragon of fear that holds men back, tied to their materialism and their despair?

This Master was sent to France to spread the solar Teaching of the Great Universal White Brotherhood (white for Light as opposed to darkness, Universal for the Sun). He was given this mission by his Master, Peter Deunov, who was born in Bulgaria, land of great Initiatic traditions safeguarded by the Bogomils, themselves the forerunners of the Templars, the Cathars and the Albigensians. Originally there were nine Knights Templar, whose goal was to install a government by Synarchy: Hugues de Payns, Godefroi de Saint-Omer, André de Montbard, Gundomar, Godefron, Rozal, Geoffroy Bisol, Nivard de Montdésir and Archambaud de Saint-Aignan. They were sent as emissaries to Jerusalem, to King Bodoin I; the Pope, along with Peter the Hermit, was stirring up the Crusades. What history does not tell is that Hugues de Payns and his friends passed through Bulgaria on their way to Constantinople and Jerusalem. The Bogomils were then at the height of their power, encouraged in their erudition and esoterism by King Simeon the Great, who put all Sages, Prophets and Mages under his protection leaving them free to read, translate, and write down all the existing Initiatic Works. Hugues de Payns and his companions were tremendously influenced by the Bogomils. They changed, and committed themselves to work for the good of mankind... which is why the Templars, Cathars and Albigensians were persecuted from then on (1307) by the Church and by Philip IV. The Order of the Temple was founded in 1118 ; it was rescinded in 1312 by Pope Clement V. All the leading Knights Templar were burned at the stake, including Jacques de Molay, in 1314. In Bulgaria, the same thing was happening to the Bogomils who were massacred and burned alive, because they were a nuisance to the kings and powerful boyars who spent their time feasting and amusing themselves... and oppressing the people. Many of the Bogomils succeeded in escaping from Bulgaria, and took refuge in Italy, France or England. They were in a pitiful state of poverty and misery. The French mispronounced their name, which became «bougres» (bulgarian, bulgars, buggers), so that now a bougre means someone who is poor and miserable. And there is also the story of Esclarmonde de Foix, who was consumed with passion for a Bulgarian who had gazed upon her just once, an Initiate and Bogomil called Nicetas (in Bulgarian : Nikita). One look !


Such were the descendants of the Johannine School, the Church founded by Saint John the beloved disciple, who received the essence of the Initiatic Teaching from Jesus, while Peter received the mission to spread the formal aspect of the Teaching. As we near the end of our civilization, it is the core of the Christian era – Jerusalem and Rome – that is going to suffer. History shows that there are necessarily two currents in the Teaching of the Initiates: one visible, the Churches, Temples and Pyramids with their icons, symbols, costumes and rituals; and the other that no one knew existed, the heart of the Church, hidden and secretive, but very much alive. Some worked in the fields at the foot of the Pyramids, worshipping the mysterious power of the symbols without understanding, while others took part in the secret life within, after undergoing the most severe Initiations. Everything that we hear about the life of Peter Deunov from witnesses or from his own writings, demonstrates his belief in the inner Church of Saint John: Love ye one another, in spirit and in truth, apart from forms, badges, and appearances. As early as the First World War, this Master spread his new Teaching and his new methods, the Universal White Brotherhood, throughout Macedonia. But hadn't Jesus talked about the same thing? Hadn't Moses thought about it? And what was it that Ram taught the peoples of antiquity, what was his heroic achievement? Behold the triumphant Sun of Ram swinging back to Europe! Behold Maître Omraam Mikhaël Aïvanhov missioned by his Master with most penetrating foresight, to install the nucleus, the core of the Universal White Brotherhood, in France.

It was Svezda who offered «Brother Mikhaël» the hospitality of her apartment in Paris. She was the first to witness the daily proofs that this Master is helped by high entities in the invisible world. Having no papers to his name except the round trip ticket for the Exposition of 1937, now outdated, he had to obtain permission to remain from the authorities, giving sufficient reason for prolonging his stay, every week for two years! Svezda wrote a book about his adventures, suggesting quite clearly that there was constant action on the part of the invisible world. This kind of thing leaves most people skeptical, specially those who are behind the bars of their egocentricity and pride. How can materialists be expected to recognize the subtle world? We need ears and eyes to see in the outside world, we need qualities and special organs to see in the invisible world, without which it remains closed. Initiates have developed these organs and these qualities. With our limited field of vision, we have no right to judge them: we who have no power, how stupid of us to doubt their power! We can only see what we have been given to see. Or else we can listen to someone we trust.

Svezda was at that time an Astronomer at the Observatory, a most learned and scholarly person who had herself received when she was young and in the midst of spiritual experiments, a spiritual teaching, which she took down. One day in July, 1937, she read a book by the Bulgarian Master, Peter Deunov, «The Master Speaks». Stupefaction! It was exactly the same Teaching that she had been receiving inwardly! She left at once for Bulgaria. Master Peter Deunov received her, and told her that upon her return, she would be asked to work with someone (he didn't say that it would be «Brother Mikhaël») whom she would then serve all the rest of her life. Upon her return, a series of things happened «by chance» leading to her meeting with the Maître.

«I was still full of the excitement of my trip to Bulgaria. As soon as I saw Master Deunov's disciple, I was startled by the intense auric light that surrounded him. His inner nature resembled that of Master Deunov. While in Sofia, I had met some remarkable people among the disciples, particularly a professor at the University whose face displayed great erudition and truly exceptional esoteric, intellectual, and spiritual knowledge, but none of the disciples could compare with the one before me now. «This is a true disciple of Master

Deunov!» said a voice within me. «This is the face I was shown one day: Saint John!» Everything about him, his eyes, his hair, his expression, at once masculine and feminine, left no doubt in my mind. I was sure this was the disciple I was to work with.

«All this happened in the space of a few seconds, a lightning perception impossible to describe. I knew at once what I was to do.

«There were other revelations later on that I told Brother Mikhaël about, concerning his spiritual level, the nature of the mission with which he was charged, and the results that would be forthcoming. Events proved them correct.

«Above all, at our first meeting, it was the intense light that emanated from him that struck me, a light full of gentleness and pure impersonal love, pouring out like divine water on people and things. His look was the inner gift of himself, a total giving that belongs only to saints and Masters.

«Watching Brother Mikhaël in action, one got the impression that his only concern was to offer this divine gift of love to all and sundry, with no restriction. This was all the more noticeable because of his inability to express himself in French, it made people conscious of what emanated from him. The radiance of his spiritual love shining through his unusual beauty touched everyone who came in contact with him.

«The number of friends who wanted to hear Brother Mikhaël speak increased daily. At first we held the meetings in my apartment, but as it only held about twenty people at a time, we had to form groups and assign them to different days or evenings. Finally we found a hall in Paris where we could all come together and hear Brother Mikhaël, and even bring our friends. There was never any question of charging an entrance fee; we divided the cost of the hall. Neither then nor later did the idea ever cross our minds of making any profit. If we had, as far as Brother Mikhaël and I were concerned, we would have been going against the very basis of the spiritual life : gratuitousness.

«Around this time, when the lectures were first opened to the public, I showed Brother Mikhaël a crystal that had belonged to the Master Peter Deunov, which he had graciously given me. Brother Mikhaël took it from me with a gesture that moved me deeply, handling it with such care and respect, with so much gentleness and love, that is was plain to see how much the Master meant to him. The Master lived in the soul of the disciple. I never forgot this gesture, one that only a saint could have made.»

Another witness of the early days is Frida Theodosy, a gifted singer now devoted to teaching others, whom I have also known for years. She says the following : «During the thirty-three years that I have followed the Teaching of Maître Omraam Mikhaël Aïvanhov, I have undergone the most extraordinary and complete transformation. Nothing is left of my old way of living, my old point of view ; my habits and my ideas are totally changed... a sort of resurrection from a life that was fundamentally different. My eyes are opened on to another world so much more grandiose, vast, luminous and real, a world of unimaginable splendour! And even more important is this way of living permanently in joy, in peace, in the light...

«The Maître gives us a living example of his Teaching, he lives his Teaching. There are so many writers and professors who teach one thing and live differently... leading a double life, as it were. Whereas with the Maître, his life is pure, transparently pure, full of integrity and light, woven of sacrifice, abnegation and impersonal love for human beings.

«Miracles are not very significant», said the Maître one day. «You can heal people, you can raise the dead... but then

The Master upon his arrival in France in 1937

In 1959, prior to the Master's departure for India, appeared over his head on several occasions
and in different circumstances, the Kabbalistic sign of the SHIN, in shape like a flame, or a dove.
It is the symbol of the Holy Spirit.

The Master upon his return from India

they only begin all over again with the same faults and the same illnesses. The real miracle is to save a soul by filling it with light so that it will not sin any more; the real miracle is to teach human beings to transform hate into love.»

«Yet Maître Omraam Mikhaël Aïvanhov is not lacking in power! I don't mean his ability to read our thoughts. At the moment, as everyone knows, scientists are all involved (specially the Russians) with telepathy, or the transmission of thought. Now no one doubts that this faculty exists in certain people. But the Maître, beside that faculty which he certainly has, can also heal people at a distance, and stop a fire... or the rain. It's a known fact that great Masters who have gained control over their own thoughts, feelings and actions, can also control the four elements.

«When I first belonged to the Brotherhood, I used to go regularly to give singing lessons to some disciples who lived with the Maître in a large house nearby. One day, I arrived a little earlier than scheduled, and went to open the window and look out. What was my surprise to see the Maître sitting at a table in the garden eating lunch with a group of disciples! I had a completely erroneous idea of Masters in general, knowing only that their powers went far beyond that of ordinary mortals, and naïvely imagining that they had no need to eat or drink, or sleep. I shut the window and sat down to reflect on the fact that a Master needed food, just as we did.

«A little while later the door opened and the Maître came in. He sat down beside me and said: «A Master needs to eat, drink, and sleep just as everyone else does. The difference is that he is in control of his cells, he gives the orders, and his consciousness is much wider, that's all.» He went on to give me a true picture of a spiritual Master.

«Another day I was clumsy enough to make an awkward movement and sprain my ankle. I felt a sharp pain in my leg... so sharp that I could neither walk nor remain standing. Someone went to tell the Maître while others carried me home, for I could not step on my foot. Once home, still in great pain, I lay down, preparing to spend several days in bed. I noticed that it was ten o'clock. At that precise instant I felt a strange sensation in my leg and all pain ceased abruptly. I got up at once and walked on it and still felt no pain. My surprise was complete. «It doesn't hurt any more», I thought. «What a miracle!» The ankle was, in fact, comulkely healed.

The next day after the Sunrise at St.Cloud, I went up to the Maître and said: «Thank you, Maître, for healing my leg!» The Maître answered: «I'm sorry I couldn't get to it before ten o'clock, something else kept me until then.»*

I didn't want to try to describe Maître Omraam Mikhaël Aïvanhov, the solar Magus, without including the impressions of his first followers, and the things that happened, the surprising facts so difficult for our reasonable, logical minds to accept... our limitation, alas! They are worthy of faith.

But the important thing is that this Master came to France to try, against all opposition, to start the Great Universal White Brotherhood, now, at this time, in this spiritually underdeveloped epoch. That is the miracle! The solar Mage's miracle.

The Great Universal White Brotherhood! The great dream. Reminding one of all the wasted time and effort... and talk... spent on forming brotherhoods, united and indivisibly in favour of a just and lasting peace that never came! One wonders why these great Beings so close to the heart of the matter and so aware of the misery of our hearts, were unable to install the promised Brotherhood on earth before? Or why, if they wanted to and tried to, did their attempts fail? The

* Translated from the French: «L'Art du Chant Italien», by Frida Theodosy (Prosveta Editions).

answer is clear: a Brotherhood for the people can't be formed without the people! Without us! We use the word brotherhood, but what does it mean to us? What are we thinking about? About other things entirely, you know that. About ourselves, about our needs and greeds, our getting ahead and our badges, our violence and our cheating, our bungling and our blackmailing. And because of these things we think about, we make the Brotherhood deviate from its original ideal, we limit it and submit it to the form and appearance that suits us, we corrupt its heart, we desecrate it with our actions. Turning it into a common market. This is the state of things all over the earth. That is why each time the Initiates come to talk to us about Brotherhood, they are met with corruption, divergence and disagreement, irreverence and sacrilege, in society, in brotherhoods, in schools, in the past and now. When Ram fled Europe for India, he was fleeing the divergence, corruption and sacrilege of the masses. What did Moses discover when he came back down from the heights of Mount Sinaï? What condemned Jesus? The divergence, corruption and sacrilege of the masses! They preferred Barabbas. And do to-day. All civilization has moved away from its spiritual source, the heart of brotherhood, the Christ. Everything is profaned, deviated, corrupted, in art, science and politics, in cultural centres, in historical monuments, in great cathedrals... everything is polluted everywhere, in the water and in the air and in our splendid environment... is it surprising that the Initiates of history are also subject to the divergence, corruption and profanation of the majority?

It was perfectly natural for the heroic crowds that followed Ram across the world to give expression to their love and admiration and devoted fraternalism, he was the saviour, the healer of souls and bodies. It was perfectly natural for the crowd that followed Moses through the desert to give expression to their love, admiration, and fraternal feelings. He had delivered them from the yoke of the Egyptian oppressors. He

healed them in body and in soul. To-day also it would be natural for people around a Master who has saved them from
misery, from divergence, corruption, and desecration, to express their love, their devotion and their fraternalism by offering him their hearts to love and their hands to work, asking
no reward other than a look from the Master, the look that illuminates, warms, revives, vivifies and restores them to a
state of harmony with God... well, not at all, the impotents
whose only power is the force of numbers don't like that, they
refuse, and they let you know it in no uncertain terms.


The Initiates have the same power as their ideal and model, the Sun! They are solar magicians. They know their model is all-powerful, they know they can count on the future
because of their ideal. They know the time is approaching
when their ideal model's omnipotence will prove itself more
forceful than the force of numbers. It will be «on earth as it is
in Heaven». They know their «magic» will then prevail
against all the rest, they will have the upper hand and give
mankind an example of Universal Brotherhood. From the
Sun will come the heart, form and meaning of Universal
Brotherhood; from the Sun will derive its anatomy, physiology, and psychology. You will see that these words are not
mere abstractions.

To-day man varies his philosophy, policy and economics
from day to day as the situation presents itself with ever-
increasing frequency, as the inevitable, foreseeable catastrophe gets nearer and nearer. The Initiates started long ago
to prepare their solar revolution, to work for their sacred and
historic vision of the destiny of mankind. To use words that
are familiar and that I understand, now that I am part of an
Initiatic and esoteric School, the Universal Brotherhood will
be like its solar ideal, Socialistic, Capitalistic, Communistic,
Cosmic, and Synarchic! Socialistic as the Sun is Socialistic,

because it will put universal survival ahead of individual interests; Capitalistic as the Sun is Capitalistic, in that it will amass and hoard all the powers of survival in the Universe; Communistic like the Sun in the distribution of its capital (survival) to the entire community with impartiality, honesty, and justice; Cosmic like the Sun, for through this Universal Brotherhood (the example), man will be recreated and reintegrated into his rightful, initial, Initiatic environment; and Synarchic like the Sun in that it will conform in its entirety to the solar archetype, its unique authority and point of reference. In short, the Kingdom of God and His Justice as promised by the Initiates!

To-day in France, the Initiatic and esoteric School of Mâitre Omraam Mikhaël Aïvanhov is organized along the lines of the solar archetype in heart, form and meaning. The Solar Revolution has begun...

CHAPTER IV

# THE INITIATIC AND ESOTERIC SCHOOL OF MAITRE OMRAAM MIKHAËL AÏVANHOV

*FIRST, THE HEART:*
*The Solar Revolution*
*or The New Romanticism of Aquarius.*

The first thing one notices when entering the Master's School, is the way these men and women look at you, the solar look. There is no doubt about it, something joyful is going on in their hearts, something real, not fake. I know, for I am here. I might even say they have no desire to live their lives any other way. Ask them! Is it the presence of the Maître? I don't think so. Human nature is such that even a fabulous Master, a venerated Master, becomes after a while like the Sun in the sky, something accepted and normal. Besides which, the happiness of a thousand people living in the presence of a Master, be he Regent of the whole world, is very little when you think of all the people who are **not** there, who are dying of hunger, or fear. Happiness in the form of a challenge would not be my idea of brotherhood. There must be more to it than that. And here it is: all I can say is that they know they are participating in history, they know they are launching a revolution which will mean happiness for mankind, delivery from hunger and prison and heartsickness. An historic revolution. It only takes one person, or one thousand, to begin.

To start with we were only a handful, and our land was a burning desert in the wastes of Esterel, with no water, no electricity, no conveniences, scarcely a tree and no more than tumbledown ruins in which to set up our tents. We were here to work, and we sweated. It was no easy refuge, no sanctuary close to a Master. And still less so to-day. But it has become civilized, the camp is organized. The caravans and mobilhomes have running water and electricity and cooling ventilators, there are loudspeakers in the trees that circulate celestial music throughout the camp; there are flowers everywhere; the paths are covered with asphalt; there is ample parking; the farm machinery hums pleasantly; our own printing press turns out the Master's books; the bakery gives us fresh baked bread and hot croissants; we drink the wine of our own vineyards; everything is there, sanitary installations, dormitories, modern kitchens, special chalets for art, for music. The children have their own refectory, their own corner for games, art and music. Truly, nothing is missing. And there is the lecture Hall, sacred as a Temple, a cathedral of light, where each one comes and contributes his silence. We know that one day we will have a university, an Initiatic University. And when I come here in summer, I know that I am not coming to a place of refuge. No. Nothing is organized here for that. On the contrary, the Master knows better than anyone how to put people to work, how to make them do their utmost, and how to draw the best out of both people and circumstances. He will dare anything to keep his Initiatic School from appearing as a shelter, with himself the reception committee (which, I repeat, would be very little). It is simple: he knows how to make the basic currents circulate in such a way that each person is caught up in them, involved, restrained and compelled to reconsider himself unceasingly (some of our friends have left). What he wants to do is to **prepare a revolution in thought!** A basic and radical reorganization of our way of thinking. Which is quite different from a privileged fraternity far removed from the oil slick. Otherwise it doesn't make sense. It does make sense once you understand what the Master is trying to do : train and fit people to recognize their own power and capacity, and show them how to avoid things that can limit or weaken them : all sensory, intellectual and educational prejudice, all preconceived ideas and habits no matter how pleasant that make us stand still and keep us from seeing the real wonders. Yes, if you understand the solar revolution that is beginning to stir in the world to-day, you will understand the Master's wish to develop and prepare a new man. That is what makes hearts happy at the Master's School. It is all they think about : Solar Revolution and the creation of a new type of man.

At the moment men's minds are taken up with the scientific revolution. We talk interminably about data processing, about the future when everything will be done by computer, when all the knowledge, learning, skill and science that the human mind has acquired or invented since time began will be stored, processed and programmed. Man will no longer need to use his brain to work with, or his heart to love with, his daily requirements will also be stored, processed and programmed, including death, since his Bomb is already stored, processed and programmed for death. That is the future imagined by pundits, philosophers and political leaders, since that is the extent of their information, their data.

There is however other, more glorious data, solar data, that was «stored, processed, and programmed» by the Cosmic Spirit thousands of years ago. Christian information. Compared to which, how little is worth any information from the uninformed human mind ! Here it is, this data, in all its visible and poetic beauty :

... Blown by the autumn winds on to a pile of leaves and manure, the seed of a flower takes root for the winter in cold and darkness. In the spring it bursts into bud ; in summertime it flowers; and then it gives its seeds to the autumn wind on a pile of leaves for a new flowering, no matter what, regardless of war and strife, regardless of man. It is a fact. It is the proof that the Sun preserves the life of the daisies in the field, to the rhythm of seasons as contradictory as night and day, but through which everything moves to its flowering!...

Well, I don't believe any more in lost futures, regardless of war and strife, regardless of men. Our flowering is our survival. That is what the solar data announces, the information that our human data processing forgets to give us. We are all, flowers and men, in the same cosmic bath, are we not? Therefore, if we sense that things are beginning to change in the world, we can write down without fear that the change is in order to permit a new flowering, a new civilization that will provide us with a new flowering! That is the dominant fact in the history of man; it alone can throw a light on the bewildering contradiction of our tides and eddies. A flowering! Regardless of war and strife, regardless of man. With it, because of it, everything becomes transformed and magnified as it moves toward further magnificence for all species and realms ever since the beginning. That is what raised man to a vertical position, made him stretch his thinking heart toward Heaven, and use his imagination to see ahead, to what his history would be. The only one who could! Raised to his feet in order to imagine and create his solar future. The only one who could store, process and distribute the solar information. The only one who could! Why not do it? Why not live in the certitude that the path to our natural flowering leads on to a marvellous future, not too far off, at least for those who think of nothing else. Which is the case here, in this School. With a Master who is the immarcescible example. That is our Initiation into an Initiatic School. Knowing that the flowering is not far off. Living it now. A new way of life, beginning at dawn. A way of rising from the ashes. A new, reviving way of thinking. A revolution of the mind: **the solar revolution of mentalities.** When they talk about it, the children of the XXIst Century who already live it in their hearts, they will really wonder why the men of the past, the pundits, philosophers and politicians, thought about anything else. Those who are part of the resurgence, the new life, the new earth, the new attitude and the new behaviour, will shed a tear for the man of the XXth Century who lived and died without ever glancing up at Heaven.

This is the time when the vernal point is about to enter Aquarius, the sign of a new flowering for men of good will. In the heavens above the clouds, all around the Sun, extraordinary things are going on. New cosmic currents are circulating around the earth. Everything is moving, you can see it, each one feels it in his heart, in families and societies and countries. There is no escaping it. The new flowering is a scientific, astronomic fact, quite easy to understand.

The earth moves around the Sun in three* distinct movements: a daily movement that determines the days and nights; an annual movement that determines the seasons; a secular movement that determines civilizations and occurs every 2,160 years,** the length of time it takes for the vernal point to go from one sign of the Zodiac into the other. Each time it happens, the Cosmic currents burst forth with new sap, new vigour, for the new flowering. There is no escaping it. Each time it happens it means new life for realms and species, each time, men's brains are reconditioned by the new currents. We are not the same in the morning as we are at

* Actually a single spiralling movement that includes all three.

** The vernal point takes 72 years to go one zodiacal degree; it takes 72 times 360, or 25,920 years to cover the entire Zodiac; it takes 12 times less than that to go from one sign of the Zodiac to the next, or 2,160 years... the duration of a civilization.

night, we are not the same in summer as we are in winter, nor are we to-day what we were 10,000 years ago. Yes, everything is changed, transformed by this play of cycles in time : the cycle of days that renews life, the cycle of seasons that renews the flowers, and this secular cycle that renews civilizations. The Universe thus assures its own survival by renewing life, renewing the flowers, renewing civilizations. To-day, the earth is passing from the cyclic season of Pisces to the cyclic season of Aquarius. The renovation of civilization ! The defeat of entropy ! A fresh start for man's mind ! A flowering ! There will be those who don't understand (their minds have been on other things) and they will be distressed, distressed to death perhaps. There will be others who will be infinitely glad.

On the path of history, you can already see the new flowering and feel the new currents. Look :... in the beginning of the Christian era (the cycle that began two thousand years ago and is now coming to an end), the seed of our civilization, planted by Jesus, grew like a flower. With Christ, the Solar Spirit came to dwell in the heart of the centuries. Christ, the example, the criterion, the circuit, the centre, worshipped by the whole family, at home, talked about as they ate their bread and wine, in remembrance. In his Name, they built the world's beautiful cathedrals, studied his life and sayings in universities, governed society. A trade or profession that went against his Name in any way was not acceptable ; nor were dealers, speculators, exploiters, perverted instructors or politicians, any who deviated from the sacred or desecrated his holy Name... the violent, the dishonest, the tricksters. The arts flourished. Even wars were fought in his Name, proof that the Powers knew they needed him ! It lasted all through the Middle Ages, up to the Renaissance... a story of love, of the heart, of miracles taking place in the marketplace amid the bread and the cheese, of village churches built by every-one wielding shovels together, of love... the subject of songs, love, the cause of wars between the countries of Europe; love and womanhood, the inspiration of man. Knights were the example men followed, knighthood was their aspiration. It was a time of chivalry, courtliness and gallantry, of ballads and poetry and romance, of Lancelot and the Holy Grail. A beautiful flowering! Alas! With the natural phenomena of entropy inevitably following behind, the epoch wore itself out. Came the era of philosophy, introducing doubt into the spirit of things. Encyclopedists questioned the established principles, faded with age.* Next it was the turn of philosophy to wear itself out. The scientific movement came in as electric lights lit up the last century. Like a rose at the end of summer, the flower came to life again just as it was beginning to fade, its sap used up, its spiritual, philosophic, and moral fibre worn down, the vitality of the family and the bourgeois, wea-kened. Nothing remained but the economic appearance, neon lights, a sure protection against time and entropy. Or so we thought. It was an illusion. To-day nothing is left standing, it is all shifting and disintegrating.

But a decaying flower is also the promise of a new flower-ing. Wonder of wonders! The new Age promises to be exactly

* Author's note: The XVIIIth Century, the century of light, and «French Europe» are what changed history, along with the movement of de-Christianization in the West. At the same time, French literature, with widespread influence, began to criticize the existing establishment and its traditions. The idea of Economics emerged out of the current morality and philosophy (or rather, began to emerge... actually it will have to wait until the XIXth Century). At the same time an explosion of demography over-threw conventional society. It is a time of expansion, as man seeks liberty and moves away from the enclosed heart of things to the periphery and the surface. The century ended with two strokes of lightning that released the new and violent currents we are still feeling the backlash of to-day: the French Revolution, and the American Declaration of Independence. The tides of Aquarius!

as the Initiates have described it : Aquarius pouring out onto the world (and into our hearts) the life-restoring Cosmic currents.

We can see the same currents in the rebellion of the youth of to-day, bent on destroying the old forms and liberating the spirit of things... to live! They may be going about it the wrong way, but they are doing it. They feel like participating in their Universe; they become ecologists. They feel like escaping from the narrowness of the intellect: they become manual experts and make their own bread and wine jugs. They feel like breaking away from the bourgeois limitations of their education: they become liberated. They feel like studying the possibilities of the psychic life and abolishing all borders: they live in communities. It occurs to me that what they really want is space. Inner space, space to breathe, space for brotherhood, space for love! Aquarius going into action! The new currents! In the symbolism of the Zodiac, Aquarius corresponds to February, when the seed that was sown earlier appears above ground and becomes part of the environment. It needs space, it needs to communicate, with its flowering in mind. We are, in effect, moving toward space and communication between each other, between us and our Universe, and it is certain that everything closed in (confinement in sects, couples, families, and society) is doomed. The Planet Uranus which governs Aquarius, is responsible for the spasmodic agitation and vibrations of this era of communication: telephone, telegraph, radio, television, wavelength, satellite, telepathy, and thought; exploration of the brain and PSI powers; rockets to the Moon, to Mars, to Venus... the grasping of subtle forces... etc. And the Lion, in the axis of Aquarius, is responsible for the magnificence and the generosity of the new ideas, beginning in 1789, with the adoption of the Phrygian cap, the emblem of Liberty, borrowed from Ganymede, the Aquarian Sage who pours out the water! Water is the life of the earth! It flows and the flowers come up. And since life is in essence solar, the new flowers are bound to be solar. Away with lunar philosophies! As opposed to the benighted era of Pisces, now making its exit, with its secret inquisitions and tragic and mute Initiations (I am thinking of the Bogomils, the Albigensians, the Templars, all part of the Church of St. John). As opposed to the gloom of the last days, as opposed to the seizure of power away from man, the new Age will be one of freedom and joy, burning with the fire of the Spirit (foreseeable because of the play of opposition with which life maintains its balance through the changing seasons). As opposed to materialism, the new Age will be spiritual. If not, how would it be new? Ridiculous, today's politicians, talking about a «new society» with the same old jargon, the same materialistic point of view! Impossible! The new Age will be the age of spirituality. Not the frozen, ascetic, aseptic, asexual spirit of the unenlightened Pisces, but of Spirit, liberated by the fire of imagination! Man will **imagine** his grandiose future. There. And the spiritual truth will prevail against the popularization of science that we are told to accept as the only reality, against the diploma, the profit-taking, and the things we are sold, and accept as the only reality. As opposed to the actual confusion, it will bring us a precise policy that will have the life, the love, the laws of Heaven for model. And each heart will imagine its own solar future, as the only way to liberate man and make him brotherly. The new solar forces will break down our sensitivity, our susceptibility, barriers will give way, inhibitions will disappear, complexes, shame and superstition will melt into the past, and new cells will open up along with new possibilities. Above his intellect (which is merely analytical) man will feel his intuition beginning to waken, a sort of sixth sense, with the faculty of immediate perception and synthesis. The pineal gland in flower! The corolla found in our superior, vertical mammal... man! The thousand-petaled lotus, as it is called. The natural consequence of the evolution of the heart, pursuing the solar revolution, demonstrated by the manifestation of other needs, inner, more subtle needs. Instead of being chained to the world of objects which absorbed us until now, we will be free! Our need now is for quality in life, we are thirsty for something different : for the Sun! Ask people in the street whether they don't feel a need in their hearts for something that would be like the Sun... something that would warm and encourage them. And if that is so, ask them if they would not like to meet Someone, from here or from anywhere else, who carries the Sun in his heart.


**As opposed to the mediocrity of our age, the new Age will be romantic!**


Don't be misled by the word «romantic» and its current interpretation. Romanticism is not as it is generally thought to be, pallid and wan, vague and distraught; it has nothing to do with sentimental wanderings, or marijuana, or intellectual ravings, or the neurotic romanticizing of the moment, or the «romanticism» of modern thinking, in defiance of the Sun. No. It is rather, it is in fact, the great Cosmic story! It means accepting to live consciously, the change of seasons, participating in the change rather than staying behind in the cold, sad, archaic, winter. The Cosmic story, or history, is «romantic» in that it belongs to tradition, to the beginning, to the traditional chivalresque initiative of the Initiates. «Romantic» is the word for the kind of literature that was inspired by the spirit of chivalry and the idealistic knighthood of Medieval Europe. Having to do with heroes, with virtue and grandeur. Having to do with us, the solar mages. Having to do, to-day, with the Golden Age, the Age that we proclaim in song and verse, immortalizing deeds of valour and high idealism. The Age that will be here before the end of the century, as our hearts have been told for so long by the Initiates. Proclaim the Age to which we all aspire! The Age of happiness, of no more wars, of no more poverty or suffering, of no more criminals or prisons, of no more frontiers or walls, of no more inquisitions, or divergence, or corruption, or sacrilege! The Age when all men will love each other, as brothers.

# THE INITIATIC AND ESOTERIC SCHOOL
# OF
# MAÎTRE OMRAAM MIKHAËL AÏVANHOV

*SECONDLY, THE FORM:*
**The Brotherhood That Took The Sun For Model.**

The second thing that hits one upon arriving at the Maître's School is the life there. Or rather, the feeling one has of penetrating into another life. Becoming immersed in it. Here the air vibrates differently, not only because of the Sun and the song of crickets, but because of the surprising realization of one's own weight, a heaviness that comes from the bad habit of thinking about other things. Until, of a sudden one beautiful morning, the heart opens up and you understand. I put it into words: this School has the Sun as its model. Yes, now, to-day, as we step into the 1980's, we are offered another life, a solar life! To live it is possible... I have done it. Not on some other planet with creatures from outer space, but here in France, on the ground, the good ground of the Bonfin, on the Riviera near Fréjus. And if one day someone actually comes from outer space to land their flying saucer among the pink oleanders on the field where the great bonfire is held each year at Michaelmas... I think the astonishment will be on their part. They will be surprised because a Brotherhood that has the Sun for model is a surprising thing, unique in the world. No less than a solar revolution!

This solar organization* is being realized in France by

* Volumes XXV and XXVI, Complete Works, O.M.Aïvanhov.

Maître Omraam Mikhaël Aïvanhov to such a high degree of scientific, pedagogical, historical and esthetic pureness, one wonders why people, the learned, the knowledgeable, the educators, philosophers and politicians, don't avail themselves of it. Is there anything more brotherly than the Sun with its great and good heart? I repeat, the Sun gives to everyone, to each and every one of us without discrimination, segregation, inquisition, bargaining, harrassment, rebuff, frustration, disgrace, and... without remuneration, distributing freely a wealth of calories for our physical survival and making available to us the three sources of happiness: light, love, and life. With such a profusion of joy in springtime, such extravagance of beauty, form, colour, fragrance and song, such enchantment, that if we do not say «thank you», we must really and truly be thinking of something entirely different; to put it flatly, we must be no more than an animal, a slob. And look, here is a model that will never wear out, never be subject to corruption, deviation, vulgarity, sacrilege, uncertainty, fatigue, or illness. Do you realize that there are scientists and scholars in America to-day who can see nothing but illness and crime and ugliness wherever they look? they discovered recently that the Sun has some illness or other, and now they are waiting for the Sun to die! Would you believe it? Fools may come and fools may go, but the Sun is here forever!

The Sun can never be turned aside by evil thoughts, nor corrupted by evil hearts, nor desecrated by evil actions. The Sun is immarcescible. Nothing is higher! What a wonderful brotherhood we could form together on earth! It would be fabulous! Well, I am witness to the fact that here in France, there is a Master who is making that effort. In his grandeur and patience, his suffering even, due to this monstrous age (an organism is monstrous when there is mal-conformation), this Master wants to prove to all men of good will that there exists a way of living collectively (the only way to live happily, fully, in perfect health... psychically) available to all, every race, every colour, every creed, every sect, every origin and condition... providing all are united in the same good will, no more than that, «that» being enough to do away with all war, all ruins, all frontiers and all poverty. «That» being what would permit the Cosmic forces of Communism and Capitalism, both necessary, to work together (instead of destroying each other) toward the same flowering, by capitalizing solar energy and then distributing it to the community in the form of fragrance and colours, flowers and fruit. A dream of Brotherhood, what. Yes, I bear witness to the fact that it is taking shape, this Brotherhood that stems from the magic of genius, the solar mages. And when I watch a Master at work on the material realization of this dream (already a fact), I am obliged to conclude that no learned men, no philosophers or political leaders will ever be able to present brotherhood to mankind until they can radiate brotherhood in their hearts, visibly, as the Master does. That is the difference. You agree that all is said, all has long since been said (and done) on the subject of brotherhood, in dissertations, books, and oratory (and the guillotining of heroes) except one thing, surprisingly: that it begins with the heart. Primarily, before anything. For the Master, the Brotherhood is the preliminary flowering, the innate power of the heart, and he has the ability to awaken that power in men's hearts. That is his power. Besides the power, he has the knowledge, the patience, and the love, and has had for more than thirty-five years! I am here to testify! He has the heart for it, and it is so that we also will have the heart for it, that his School is patterned on the solar heart. He creates the atmosphere.

It's true that men talk about brotherhood, but they don't know how to create atmosphere. They really do think about other things all the time (since nothing is realized), about how to obtain money and possessions and pleasure... material things. They build palatial Market Centres with food, fashion, cars, banking, household appliances, all very helpful when we need money and material things, but what about the heart? What about Brotherhood? Have you ever wondered why there is no «Heart and Brotherhood Centre»? Isn't it odd that there is no market for what we lack most? No, the right atmosphere is lacking for we create other conditions. Cause and effect: the heart gives in, subsides, and fainting, falls to its knees, wasted away. How can it be expected to flower?

Here at the Initiatic School, the difference is the Master: he begins with brotherhood. With the Idea of Brotherhood. It's all he thinks about. He creates the conditions. The solar atmosphere! Nothing to do with the usual, the ordinary symposiums, reunions or conferences. Here the currents circulate from the heart, not from objects, and so the miracle is accomplished: Cause and effect!* The disciples find themselves quite naturally revived, bathed and stimulated by the currents of force of this natural, inspired, organization. In the solar atmosphere, they can open their hearts to the inner spaces of the new romanticism... of Aquarius. That is the light you see reflected in their eyes when they look at you... the first thing you notice upon entering this School. They live differently. The life is different. It is solar!

One can't put everything down in detail. One can only make an outline. I have already described elsewhere the way

* Author's note: It should be noted that the Initiates hold as most important the law of cause and effect that governs the Universe and forces itself on our hearts. You reap what you sow, it's as simple as that. A cosmic and unalterable law, not a changeable and ineffective human law, easy to avoid. Cosmic laws cannot be escaped. That is why the Master I describe is concerned first of all with atmosphere and the currents of cause and effect that circulate in that atmosphere, the currents of light. See «Cosmic Moral Laws», Volume XII, Complete Works, Omraam Mikhaël Aïvanhov.

in which this organization demonstrates the policy of the World Government as it will be before the end of the century, according to the Initiates. What I would like to bring out is... I was going to say the method, and it is a method, but it is primarily an Achievement. I am convinced that this Master is making History. He is preparing the Great Work. He will present it. He already is presenting it, so that it can increase and multiply in the world. I am thinking about this «increase and multiply». It was not connected with dependents' allowances. Jesus was not advocating large families or encouraging mammalian appetites. He was attempting to inspire our imaginations, our particular power, so that the impulse to love one another might increase and multiply. If the world is to be saved, to-day, it will not be by a band of disciples, even led by Jesus himself, but by the Great Work, rightly understood and multiplied. It will be done quite naturally, by groups of young people all over the world, by the ones who come here to learn, by the ones who listen to what they have to say when they return to their countries, and by all whose hearts are inspired, even at great distances. Thus, one fine day, there will be thousands of Brotherhood Centres built on the same lines as this one, forming all together a single collective body. At that time there will be no stopping people from talking about Universal Brotherhood. Ram is supposed to have done that, sending his emissaries out into the world as a sample of his Teaching. I think that is the way to do it; I don't think it can be done any other way. So many have attempted! God! And still no peace, no brotherhood.

Now it will be the youth of Aquarius who will do the talking. No longer will they let themselves be fooled, no longer will they believe in falsehoods, absurdities, or downright impossibilities. Once they know a solar model of Brotherhood exists, they will have one thing only in their hearts: the desire to do it, to dare to realize it. That is why, having had the unbelievable privilege of participating in the realization of this first model of the Initiatic and Esoteric School of Maître Omraam Mikhaël Aïvanhov, I am conscious of the importance of my role of writer, as the recorder, and it makes me proud.


The first thing this Master does, then, is to create a solar atmosphere for his School. It is a powerful atmosphere. «There is a secret you should know, which is part of the Initiatic philosophy. If you don't know this secret, this truth, whatever you may do, however much you may study and learn and whatever you become... writer, scientist, artist, musician, Head of State, etc... there will always be something lacking, the one thing you need in order to know the truth and understand life, people, and all the rest. The secret is, there are three worlds: the world of principles, the world of laws, the world of occurrence and action. Or, in other terms, the divine world, the spiritual world, and the physical, material world. Or, the worlds of meaning, of content, and of form, or appearance.»*

The Master's School is actuated by these three worlds. The secret is there. The solar model in three worlds. Light, love, life! Light is the core of the organization. Love is the fruit. Life is the visible physical activity, the multicoloured outer skin. What a wealth of information for the scientists, philosophers and politicians!

* Author's note: Light, love (warmth), life: the order of the Creation. From the subtle to the dense. The same order for condensation, and the materialization of energy (formation of the atom). There is also the inverse order, the dense going toward the subtle, the order of the sublimation of things, and the dematerialization of energy (disintegration of the atom). Alchemists condensed these two Cosmic processes in the words «Solve et Coagula». One might also say that in the spiritual world, things go from light (thought) to life (movement, realization, action), and that in the material world, things go from movement to light, the reverse. A guide for the course to take, depending upon whether the goal is to concretize the idea of brotherhood for mankind or to sublimate the idea in men's hearts.

The fact that the School has been founded on the three worlds of light, of love, and of life gives it its particular radiance, a quality peculiar to the invisible world. «How light the air is here!» And the further one goes into the subtle aura of this School, the more one is obliged to recognize (with emotion) that it is a question of the Maître's aura also, the aura of the Initiate whose heart is the soul of the organization. A reflection of solar power! For men of good will this discovery can be moving and upsetting beyond anything you can imagine... a secret discovery that will transform one person into a thing of beauty, and make another take to his heels. «How wonderful!» they murmur, round-eyed (I have seen it), and then they slip away and disappear completely as though nothing had ever happened. They are afraid.

The thing is that these three words denote adventure. A series of events will be set off by the force of the currents, and that is the time the decision will have to be made whether to go or stay. Actually we will have to stay, there is no escape, for the adventure is an inner one, an adventure in which we are involved in spirit and in truth, in flesh and blood, without a possibility of extricating ourselves. There are three worlds to cross, three worlds within us. The genius of Maître Omraam Mikhaël Aïvanhov is that he makes us aware of them. By the solar atmosphere. Not only mentally aware, not by intellectual knowledge, but lived and felt with all our heart, with pain and with joy. We laugh and we cry. That's life! Our inner life, with a vision of happiness at the end. Nothing to do with any political, sentimental, or personal idealistic dream... that kind of dream does not lead to brotherhood. Here is a Brotherhood of the heart, imagining its solar future in order for it to come true... under those conditions, yes, it is an adventure that alters a man's life.

One day, it will alter the life of mankind. The force of circumstances will make all men feel the need to abandon the childish and theatrical quarrels that line them up on opposite sides, left team against right team, ideological teams, economic teams, geographic teams, teams that win by cheating, all of them aggressive. When men do feel that need, then the most intelligent and the most awakened of all the Heads of State will stand up and say the words they are waiting for: there must be a new world order, new universal thinking. But none of that can happen unless we live in the three worlds that animate the Universe: the world of light, the world of love, the world of life.

### 1. The World of Light

Imagine, if you will, the first streaks of light at dawn above the silver grey waters of the Mediterranean. Imagine a crowd of people sitting in silence, wrapped in blankets against the cold of the first few moments. Waiting. The Sun is about to rise. And with the Sun, the world of light. Everything will be tainted pink, orange, tangerine, the air will be fresh and sweet, fragrant with wild thyme and marjoram. The feast! Inside me is a permanent memory of those shimmering moments that put a seal on my life. The Sun climbs the sky. You watch. You love. You receive. You imagine the Sun inside you. You say to yourself that the Sun is your model. You try. The first miracle! Cause and effect! You are filled with a sense of well-being! As each seed has a flower to give, so in the heart of each man of good will who is present at the Sun's rising, rise new forces, forces coming, the Initiates say, from the heart of Heaven! No trifling thing! Filling us with life! It is Prâna, the subtle etheric force known in India since the beginning of time (now beginning to be discovered by our scientists) that guarantees our biological survival on earth. It is present in the negative molecules of the atmosphere at dawn. Without it life would be finished, there would be no life. Along with it, the most forceful Force of all forces as Hermes describes it in his Emerald Tablet, is the spiritual Force called Telesma,* the primary force, the force of the beginning, the source of all force, the force that keeps the Universe alive, continually springing forth out of Cosmic Spirit. The force that has always chased away death, since life still exists, that chases away all illness, weakness, difficulty! It would take volumes for all of us to relate the story of our adventures in the world of light, the things each one experiences, understands, feels and lives, and the resulting spectacular improvement in his psychic and physical health... diseases cured, cells rejuvenated, organs purified, peace and strength restored. Medically speaking, what happens is that the gentle concentration on the solar image and the resulting psychophysiological nerve reaction induces a lowering of residual tension and a relaxation of cortical excitation. Meaning, in simple language, that life is beautiful and joy comes flooding back when we are face to face with Heaven! That is the adventure, the inner intellectual and emotional adventure. By renewing our ties with the sacred, we regain the great spaces of health. Cause and effect.

And there is the Maître to listen to!

I hear that warm, vibrant, reassuring voice echoing in the four corners of my heart. I have heard it so many times, coming across the clear summer air at dawn, above the Mediterranean... a lofty privilege. Biblical. Historical. A voice, a tone, an intensity, words, the Word. Some day the whole world will feel its aura, its prânic and talismanic vibration. Truth for whoever can listen to him with an open heart; truth for those who think: «This Master and I are on the same side.» Together on the same side of the Sun. For the receptive heart, yes, the voice is solar. It is beneficial as the Sun is beneficial,

* Talisman = Telesma (Greek), Tilasm (Arabic), Danichmand (Persian)

it enlightens, warms, and revives; it has the same electro-magnetic magic of space, it is protective as the dawn, searching as the Sun's rays at noon. This voice has shown me crowds of people, weeping people, happy people, transfigured people, and a thousand other people have seen it too. If some of them went away, petrified, it was because their hearts had already turned to stone. I close my eyes and breathe in this voice, it has a taste of resin and wild thyme like the place where I heard it for the first time. I can never lose the sensation it gave me, sharper than memory or imagery, more lasting than perfume or sound, it has become my own flesh and blood in the deepest part of me, my silver cord, my safe refuge and my fortress, my high house of defence. It is my origin, my secret Initiation, the mother of all that has meant happiness for me, linked with everyone I love, my brother, my Brothers, my fresh and clear-eyed girls, the ones in the past and the ones ahead shining their light on the future, making it bright. It is my morning meditation. I have heard it so often that my heart beats to that rhythm, it is the reason my heart beats, and I can say it now, O Maître, that where I feel my discipleship, where I remember most acutely that I am your disciple, is in the morning of mornings, the dawn of Summer, the sacred, historic moment when you turn around to face us and salute us with your hand, when your face reflects the Word in silence... that is the high house of defence of my life as a disciple, and to you I say, I write, THANK YOU.

The words of the Initiate have, of course, been preserved and set down. For more than forty years the Maître has been speaking to us. First on scratch pads, then on tape, his recorded words now make a considerable amount of reading matter. There is no doubt that this prolific genius speaks for history. His works show it. The books are made from notes taken down as he speaks and from recorded lectures, always improvised, and the result is that the books seem not contrived but very much alive. More than 450 works, 300 pages each, represent to-day the oral Work of Maître Omraam Mikhaël Aïvanhov, a record of the experience of brotherhood. To read it is an enlightening, warming, instructive, vivifying, happy experience. It's true! Take this one, «The Splendours of Tipheret».* You open on to a world of light, the Sun itself. The core. You find yourself at the heart of the solar revolution, wanting to rise up at once with all men of good will. You learn Surya-yoga, the yoga of the Sun, the most powerful and effective and rapid of all yogas; the most practical yoga for it can be done everywhere, in the metro, at home, at work; the most marvellous yoga in that it combats discouragement and makes us come to the surface and start the day over, it stirs the spiritual force in the cells, the psychic powers, and the imagination. Not that the word yoga is obligatory:** it is a convenience to designate the imaginary bond with the Sun, the fire, the origin. The spring. The solar discipline includes everything, every part of you is involved... head, heart, and body. It is the adventure of the future. You learn how to be alive, how to capture the Sun's etheric elements, how the Sun makes the seeds of power that have been sown inside us by Nature grow and flower. You learn why our higher Self lives in the Sun and what its power is. You learn how to find the Holy Trinity in the Sun. You learn to love as the Sun loves, to seek (and find) the Sun's protection, to fortify yourself with the Sun, to develop your aura. You become acquainted with formulas and mantras having to do with the Sun. You see why the Sun is the best Teacher of all, the Initiator of civilizations. Through this solar Initiation and the perception you gain of the Universe and its model, all the sciences are revealed... the Kabbala, Astrology, Magic, Alchemy, Medita-

---

* Volume X of the Complete Works of Omraam Mikhaël Aïvanhov.
** Yoga, from the Sanskrit = junction, link (link = religare = religion in Latin). (Yod = Bog = Gott = Dios = Dieu = GOD.)

tion... I mean «revealed», for it is this aspect of the solar re-volution that the Maître brings us: he explains quite simply the ties man has with the forces of Nature, and the Initiatic Sciences (Original Science) that until now have never been ex-plained. It was too esoteric, said the Initiates, it would be too disturbing. No one prior to this Master has ever spoken so freely and openly, or gone so far into the interpretation of the Gospels and the Apocalypse, for instance. He takes us straight to the meaning hidden within the symbols and para-bles that seemed until now so obscure and even contradictory, and we become conscious of their simplicity and their gran-deur. We realize suddenly that they are meant to reveal the close connection existing between the heart of Heaven and man's heart. Who would have thought, for instance, that the parable of the Five Loaves of Bread and the Two Little Fishes was meant to explain the power contained in our solar plexus, with seven glands in the shape of loaves and fishes and bil-lions of cells corresponding to the «filled» multitude? How do we interpret the Unjust Steward, the Five Wise and the Five Foolish Virgins? What is the meaning of «Increase and Multiply», of «Except Ye Be Converted and Become as Little Children, Ye Shall Not Enter Into The Kingdom of Hea-ven»? Whether the Master is talking about the camel who found it easier «to go through the eye of a needle than for a rich man to enter into the Kingdom of God», or any of the other parables full of depth and great truths that have re-mained obtuse for two thousand years, nothing is left out to make us understand them now. I wonder, if this Master is able to explain the Scriptures so clearly, if he is so familiar with their hidden meaning, might it not be because he partici-pated in their history? That would explain how he is able to draw from each one of these obscure texts (each one has seven meanings)*... not personal conclusions that would prove his

* See «Before the End of the Century» by the author.

intelligence and knowledge, no... but everyday things that we need in our everyday lives stated in everyday words, essential things for our health and understanding, things that bring us nearer to the source of solar life, not only by exposure to the Sun as it rises each day (which would not be sufficient in itself), but by exposure to the spiritual Sun, making us conscious of the great power of the spirit, our spirit, and the advantage of having a model, a solar model, a high ideal.* That model is lacking to-day, as you know... we may die because of it... You see how urgent it is? The awakening of the heart to its highest opportunity is called knowledge of the Self, Self-knowledge as inscribed at Delphi, Jnani-yoga. The Initiates call the solar revolution of the mind, «the second birth».** The flowering!

It is a fact that the mind certainly undergoes a change as it enters the world of light, the world of the beginning, like a field exposed to the Sun, it blossoms out. Cause and effect! I have seen it going on around me for years. The faces you see in the street are closed and hard, with lines of stress and fatigue, but here it is the opposite. Faces are transformed for the better, they gradually lose the expression they had before, eyes shine and smiles are real, reflecting a different kind of beauty, not of feature, but of spirit. A lot of charm emanates from this solar organization; it is nothing one does, but something the Sun does: the mere effort of watching the Sun rise, and then later closing your eyes and seeing it rise again within oneself creates the miracle. Cause and effect and a biological law. Call it what you will, the scientific result is there: our organs react every instant to the Sun that formed them,

* See «Life», Volume V, Complete Works, Omraam Mikhaël Aïvanhov.
** See «The Second Birth», Volume I, Complete Works, Omraam Mikhaël Aïvanhov.

making the heart radiate. A fact that is lived every morning by a thousand people of good will. Preparing them for brotherhood. This is the key to communication that we are all looking for to-day: one, sole, unique model, the same for everyone. There is no other solution. We have lived it in the praying, in the sunrise. Without that beginning, there cannot be the rest, no flowers in the fields, no birds in the trees, no flowering at all. When the Sun rises, the moment of privilege, it is the beginning that shapes the rest of the day. I know, I have missed the sunrise a few times during the summer camp, and it meant that the whole day was missed: it had no beginning, it lacked quality, finesse, light. I watched those who had gone to the sunrise as they came back down, and I sensed the higher quality of their souls. I lacked that quality. For me it was an effort to smile, to think, to will. Nothing came naturally, with secret spontaneity, as it does when your imagination is saturated, if only for a few minutes, with the image of the Sun as it rises. Brotherhood flows naturally then. Of capital importance.

They say that a novel is successful when the reader feels involved in the story himself, as though he were the hero. That happens here. The story of love is written every day, you recognize yourself in the Sun... if not to-day, then to-morrow... or the next day... early, for everything begins at dawn.

Now to show you where the Maître goes to draw his knowledge, invariably true and exact, I will give you one argument (out of hundreds). In summarizing the Teaching in the three realms of light, love, and life, I have described the world of light on the Rocher. Before going on to the world of love (warmth), I will tell you what the Maître said one day. «Can you tell me who was the first to discover, or invent, science? Or philosophy, or knowledge?» Silence. «Did the first thinkers and scholars find it mentioned somewhere?» Silence. The Maître smiled and went on : «No one will believe it, no one will accept what I am going to say, but it is the Sun who was the Initiator of science.» Silence and stupefaction. «Look at how simple it is : would anyone be able to see things, or space, or colour, or objects, or creatures, or dimensions, or be able to measure and compare them, without the light the Sun gives us? Thanks to that light man began to see, measure, learn, calculate and weigh, and pronounce himself. That is how knowledge was born. Why do men always want to know who the first one was to discover this or that? Come along further : how many people are conscious of the fact that we see? Someone will say that we see because Nature gave us eyes to see with, and not only because of the sunlight. Quite so, I reply that even children know that. But do our thinkers and scholars know why we cannot see the most important things, «invisible» things such as thoughts, feelings, life, the soul, electricity, heat, currents that circulate throughout the world, Cosmic rays, auras, vibrations, all kinds of entities and all kinds of forces? Why can't we see them?» Silence. «Because human beings are ignorant. People don't know that their eyes were formed by the Sun (whom they resemble) and that when a spiritual light is projected on invisible creatures and objects, it illuminates them, they become clearly visible to the person who projects the light! But to do that requires work and study, one must purify and sanctify oneself to become like the Sun. So, dear brothers and sisters, was it the great modern philosophers who discovered that? The greatest of attainments, the highest ideal one can have, is to become like the Sun, the Spring, the Source of life. That is my Teacher, the one who enlightens, guides and stimulates me, who helps me to improve more and more each day. Those who spend their time in laboratories and libraries studying limited and man-made inventions will never receive the essentials : light, love, and life. Is it better to be gloomy, frozen like a corpse forever? Is that the solution?»

### 2. The World of Love (warmth)

After the sunrise, we go back down the hill, buoyed up by this great feast of the heart. It's true. No one dares disturb it by speaking, even to say good morning, in order to preserve as long as possible the secret glory. At the bottom of the hill the morning has started, the Sun is already high in the sky, heat is everywhere, in the alleys of pink oleanders and in the green fields, in the song of the crickets, in the fragrance and colours. We are entering the second world of solar Initiation, the world of heat, radiance and communication. The seed bursts. The Brotherhood expands. After the secret monologue, alone, face to face with the Sun, now we are at work, thrown into the collective life like so many bees. Here the trouble begins with the clash of different temperaments, different habits, differences of background and education. And here is the second miracle! Whereas most communities wear themselves out, and so many attempts at «brotherhood» come and go or frankly fail, here, I bear witness, the Maître has had the power to «increase and multiply» his Brotherhood over a period of more than thirty-five years. However surprising the conditions may appear to outsiders, I am witness to the fact that this Master holds his disciples bound together in their hearts in spite of the disparity of their temperaments, backgrounds and habits, with such a powerful bond that it is often hard to leave the place. Later, memories come back to haunt us in the long winter evenings. The secret? This Master teaches us to see each other through the Sun, from the higher point of view. Cause and effect, always! He is himself the model in the way he looks at us: I've seen people weep for joy, unable to stand the great spaces that opened up in their hearts. «We see the Sun in each other.» Of course it can't happen all of a sudden, not in a day... perhaps not even in a whole life, but if not in this life, certainly in the next, or the one after that. That is not what counts, what counts is the effort. What counts is to know what to do, to want to do it, and to dare to go ahead in spite of our temperaments, our backgrounds and our habits. Then we can say we are really alive. We live. Life begins, as we have seen, when the Sun comes up. We've seen the pink and orange light in the sky and now we are breathing the heat of the earth, the honey. It feels good, and we say to ourselves that the others, the brothers, must be experiencing the same feeling of wellbeing. That's it, that's the beginning of brotherhood. The new mentality. Living, alive, full of life. Without the egoism of a spirituality lost in the clouds, or the abstraction of a materialism lost in concrete. This way of thinking is real and tangible, beginning in the freshness of the morning, together, and continuing in the heat of the day, together. And truly, those who have lived it know in their hearts that this is the way it will happen, the Brotherhood of all the world's peoples will begin with this gregariousness, this respect for others, this humanity. Some morning when the tribes are assembled, each one present will feel a relaxing of the solar plexus and a tightening of the roots as he discovers that they are all together in the freshness for all time, sharing the gratification of their common needs, sharing the joy of brotherhood, sharing the Sun!

Brotherhood is the need we all have not to be in the dark, not to be in the cold, not to have our dreams die like great white birds on oil-stained beaches. Brotherhood is the desire we all share not to be victims of violence, not to be exploited and cheated, brotherhood is a common taste for the opposite, a longing to become divine, to be filled with sunlight, to hear good and wonderful things that do us good. Since life is one and indivisible and we live with the same needs, brotherhood must be the need to do unto others what we would like them to do unto us. And our role, my brother, is to be the first to smile in the fresh morning air, to smile with our heart, with our glance (we the violent, the cheats and the exploiters, my

brother), to smile in the name of the Christly love we all need
so badly even if we don't dare admit it, even if all that is still
far off, for us... my brother.


See the Sun in each other! No, this is not anything that
can be arrived at quickly, neither in one day, nor perhaps in
one life, but it can be done, since the Initiate does it, since he
is the example. He has the knowledge, he demonstrates it. For
us who know that it can't be arrived at all of a sudden, that it
is extremely hard to look at each other with any sunshine and
say «Good morning, brother», as if some force in us was
holding us back... we can nevertheless see the need for Initiatic knowledge, if only to be able to live together for one instant. But we have been brought up with other things and
taught other things, such as analysis and criticism. The secret
censure is in our faces as we pass each other on the street,
chilling our features. See the Sun in each other! No, no, we
see the shadows, not realizing that when we look that way we
lose some of our life, not realizing that the dirty look we think
someone is giving us is actually our own look, not realizing
that it has a deadening effect on us, that we are obeying our
deadening nature, not realizing that we have two natures!
The knowledge that is revealed to us here constitutes another
aspect of the solar revolution of the mind, started by Maître
Omraam Mikhaël Aïvanhov.


«This knowledge,» says Maître Omraam Mikhaël
Aïvanhov, «the understanding of human nature, is the key to
the solution of all the problems of existence.» It seems to me
that he has been explaining this forever. Two forces. His disciples have assembled several lectures on this subject into a
book, an extraordinary, surprising book, the reflection of this

Initiate's Initiatic experience.* He speaks only of things he has lived and verified himself. One sees the path he took. And we see our own path now that we understand our contradictions, heretofore unbearable. Really, it all becomes clear. It is the authentic explanation of man's duality and his search for a way to be happy with his contradictory impulses.

Here... you would like brotherhood to exist, would you not? Very well, I invite you to try it. Come! You are hesitating? One half of your heart says yes, the other half says no, and you already know which you will listen to. The one that says «no» says what it wants: to be alone, to be self-sufficient, not to be bothered. Someone's coming? Hide! Hide everything (for there is always something to hide). Put on the mask! **Personality** it is called, from **persona**, the Etruscan word for a theatrical mask. The **personage** in a play. For an Initiate, it is not a good thing to be told one has personality. He knows all too well what it means. It is the part of our hearts that shows, the one that is always on stage, acting, because it is in fact weak, critical, ironic; it is lazy, always playing to the gallery, showing off, smirking, gossiping; full of excuses, fine words and beautiful emotions. Pay no attention, for if you should disturb it in any way, off comes the mask: slam-bang, like a shot, violence takes over. If you want to know where violence comes from, Mr. President, here it is! from the personality that attacks, moralizes, complains, asserts and demands, that grabs everything for itself, that throws paranoic fits, that is selfish, egocentric and interested only in itself (I have it, you have it, we all have it). That is what incites the crowds.


And the other half says yes.


* Volume XI, « The Key to the Problems of Existence », Complete Works, Omraam Mikhaël Aïvanhov.

Why are things that way? Why yes and no? Because of the duplicity of the heart. Everything at the heart, the centre of whatever it may be, is necessarily divided in two because of the two currents that cross it. Take your own heart: it has veins and arteries, one current that quickens and one that deadens; and the Sun, the heart of the Universe, has two currents, a current of life and a current of death. One current is constantly renewing life so that it will not be submerged in death due to entropy, the degradation of energy that controls the Universe: what is born must die. That's the way it is, and not to be thought of as sad, since springtime is recurrent and life always triumphs! Nevertheless, this opposition is constantly ploughing up the Universe and our hearts, caught between the current that gives life and the current that takes it away. One that gives and one that takes! Do you recognize yourself now? In every field, no matter what, be it physiology, psychology, philosophy, sociology, economics, politics, or any other, there are always two intersecting currents, one that takes and one that gives, thus making it possible for life to circulate and begin again. Always something that gives life, and something else that takes it away for its own survival. When you eat, breathe, love, make love, create, look at each other, there is always one current that gives while the other takes. It is God's miracle that He can renew life even as it exhausts itself. This universal duality explains all natural opposition, in the sap of plants and in the blood of our veins and arteries, in the sexes, in our characters, in the polarity of politics, etc... It is the basis of Initiatic knowledge. The Initiates have left its symbol everywhere: Erebe and Yona, the dove and the raven. That is why there are two opposing halves in our hearts, one half that wants everything for itself and says no to the Brotherhood, and one that renews life and its miracles by being collective.

I don't know whether this Master's Teaching is so very different from that of Jesus, of Moses, of Hermes, of Krishna, or of Ram. If I lived during those eras, I do not remember anything. Different, as to its science or its philosophy, I think not. The Initiatic Teaching, since it was there at the beginning, must be unique, ancient, permanent, continuous. I never said that this Master was bringing a new philosophy. No. His solar revolution is meant to bring a new way of communicating. And to make this possible, he creates a collectivity, for us to learn to know ourselves and to recognize the two parts of the heart, the one that says no and the one that says yes, the one that wants to take and the one that wants to give, the one that judges and analyzes in secret and the one that loves openly. The Maître is so knowing about this that he knows ahead of time how we will react. He knows that at first the «no» of the heart will tie us in knots and tighten our stomachs. «Wait three days before giving up!» he tells us, patiently. And it's true. After a while, whether by osmosis or by love, call it what you will, we begin to feel better, more relaxed, almost happy; then comes the time when we begin to appreciate the collectivity, followed by the dread of having to leave. It's true! For we have learned about the wide spaces of the heart. It is all very gradual. We realize little by little that we advance one step after the other simply because of contradictions: expansion and contraction; yes and no; the divided heart. Then we begin to understand that when we are contracted it is because of our «no», and not because of anyone else. The contractions we see in others are in reality our own contraction and opposition. When we feel that someone is aggressive, it is our own aggressivity that we feel. The stories we spread about others about sex or money prove that we have an inner conflict about those things. And the Master of this School, knowing all those things, does nothing to make it easier, on the contrary... he wants us to know about them also. He fosters opposition so that one day the heart, tired of contradiction, will free itself and spring out into heavenly space. Phew! In that way the collectivity is the quickest means of making us learn. When we manage at last to see each other across the Sun, our heart expands! It comes into its heaven! It tries to express the sublime things it feels, to spring forth in all its glory. This side, the one that says yes, the one that wants nothing but to return to the Sun whence it came, individuate, is the one called «Individuality».

Understanding the two sides of the heart, the «personality» and the «individuality», is the «key to the problems of existence». That is the science Maître Omraam Mikhaël Aïvanhov reveals to us, giving us a working knowledge of the collective life and the collective thinking, at the School or in the street. That is the revelation of the art of living together as brothers. That is, I repeat, the most important aspect of the solar revolution that will go down in Initiatic history and in the history of civilizations. I would like to point out the difference between the two words, «collectivity» and «brotherhood». One day, the Maître told us that once when everyone was meditating at Sèvres, a bird flew on to a branch of the tree nearby, and began chirping, very distinctly, the word: Troglodyte! Troglodyte! Troglodyte! Over and over! It was surprisingly clear and precise. The Maître gave a talk on the spot, from which I cite the following:

«In spite of mankind's high degree of culture and civilization, people who live together in cities, societies and families, may live a collective life outwardly, but inwardly they live apart, isolated from each other, each one thinking only about himself. That is not brotherhood. The word «collectivity» does not necessarily imply fraternity. A brotherhood is an inspired collectivity, animated by a bond with Nature that makes it both more spiritual and less selfish.»

The bird came to inspire this talk!* The Maître told us that he had travelled in several countries where people were still living in grottoes, underground, like troglodytes.

«An ordinary collectivity lacks this element of love, or brotherliness. Monks, for instance (or nuns), live in their communities together, but without love, with the pretext of being absorbed in meditation and the love of God, they remain cold and shut up within themselves. People have been burned alive in the name of God. No need to go into historical details...»

In giving us the rules of life of the Brotherhood, in giving himself as the example, the model, the Maître Omraam Mikhaël Aïvanhov fills us with real knowledge, practical knowledge that doesn't lead the mind astray or corrupt the heart, and in no way attempts to alter the will (as do the press and all news media). On the contrary, it is a magic knowledge that illuminates and warms and appeases, re-enforces,

* Author's note: Another bird in the Ile de France chirps: plus vite, plus vite! (faster, faster!) just before sunrise, as if urging people to hurry up and watch it! If you ever get up before dawn, you will hear it. Do birds utter words of themselves, or are they messengers of Cosmic currents? I leave the answer to you. When a cherry tree is in bloom, is it turning itself into a child's drawing of spring, or is it a messenger of the Cosmic currents then in action that we call Spring? I leave the answer to you. However, scientific reality wants us to believe that, living as we do, all of us in the same field of Cosmic forces, we are messengers of the invisible things that happen there, all of us, stones, vegetation, animals, humans beings. The bird did not perhaps say the word, the cherry tree doesn't perhaps realize that it is beautiful as springtime, but the message they pass on is true. Only the thing is, our descent into materialism has cut us off from this dialogue, and our conception of the invisible world is restricted to fairy tales and Walt Disney cartoons in which birds talk and... we believe in them, since we go to see them. In California there is a mocking bird that spends its time making fun of humans (nicely); they have a record of it! The Initiates are in constant communication with this invisible world, they know how to interpret the messages. How many times, for instance, has Maître Omraam Mikhaël Aïvanhov given a meaning to this or that bird in flight... and each time his interpretation or prediction turned out to be true. In antiquity, it was the Sages who had this knowledge.

strengthens, stimulates. It teaches us to look at each other with the sacred look that expresses our divine natures. Extraordinary to be able to write it, extraordinary to live it! Here we live it. No longer do we judge each other, now it's a question of helping each other. «Thou shalt love thy neighbour as thyself» by the way we look: I look at you across the Sun that is in me, I see the same Sun in you. We have the same model. That is the key! A solar model that we find on the hill of sunrises. And yes, I have received looks filled with light, I have felt the warmth of the heart, bestowed without fear. Frustration doesn't exist in that kind of climate. Don't think some monotonous and «virtuous» constraint makes us pale, pious and asexual. I wouldn't be here. It is knowing how to use the forces of love on each other, which is something else entirely, and which it is not possible to do without a knowledge of the two inner currents, the one that takes and the one that gives.

And so, on the subject of love and sexuality (the natural climate for communication between people) the Master I am talking about has given us some astounding information, answering the questions youth is faced with, explaining the need for sexual liberation, warning them about our two natures and the things that one or the other can make us experience, things as opposite as the two natures themselves. Cause and effect! (We were so sure we were headed for joy and yet we found sorrow! We all know about that.) This Master gives us most wonderful solutions... for instance, how to use our secret and powerful forces. I will not go into Tantra-yoga at the moment, but here is the essential: Maître Omraam Mikhaël Aïvanhov presents man and woman as reflections of the same Cosmic Spirit, as rays of the same light. It is because these two solar rays are differentiated, opposed and polarized on earth (so that life may circulate), that they try so hard to find each other and between them create the Sun. This need for love that lifts our hearts comes from solar radiation. The need for tenderness and affection, the need to make exchanges, the great desire to arrive at sublimation (here we are still awkward, brutal and secretive), all this realm is suddenly illuminated by... solar radiation. Is there an educator, a sexologist, a magazine on love and sex, that mentions solar radiation? So many books have been written by doctors and scientists with instructions on the technique of love... how to make love, how to get more pleasure out of it, how to... without any mention of the invisible side. What are these energies, these forces? Where do they go? What are the entities they attract? What difficulties do they provoke? etc. etc. When it is a question of anatomy, physiology and psychology, the scientific and the learned are formidable, but the Master points out their ignorance in the field of energy and emanations, of the things we attract or repulse, on the subtle etheric level. To show you how profound, original and useful is his knowledge of love and sexuality, I will give you an example in the form of a question he asked us one day: «What is love? What is sexual force?» Silence. How to answer! «It is an oil, a fuel,» said the Maître. «A special kind of fuel. The weak, the ignorant, the evil, are consumed by it, but those who know how to use it voyage in space amid the stars, using the same fuel, only using it differently, and they are not consumed, on the contrary...» Food for thought when you consider that it is the nature of our Master to verify everything he tells us. We are in danger of not being among the stars, but of falling in the first category. The Master went on, drawing us still further: «If you are looking only for pleasure in love (we have been brought up to seek only pleasure), in the long run you will find you have been robbed of your wealth and beauty, humiliated and degraded. It happens all the time. But if you go to work with this force, you will find yourself on the upswing, becoming more beautiful, richer, stronger, nobler, and in better health. The most extraordinary thing is the discovery that there can be pleasure in this way of doing things, another kind of pleasure that entails no disillusionment, no bitterness, no disgust. If one doesn't know these things, there is no doubt about it, one can end very badly...»

This kind of knowledge is nothing short of revolutionary; a solar revolution of the consciousness makes us aware that we must love. Look, do the sexologists talk this way? About chivalresque romances between princes and princesses and their joy at discovering the Sun in each other so as to bring the Golden Age on earth? We all dream, dreams make our films and cloak-and-dagger novels... but what do we live daily, how are we in our own lives? Do we live like these princes and princesses? We must read the two books on love and sexuality,* we must look more deeply into the world of our secret sultry longings, in the company of an Initiate... nowhere else will we find the answers we need.

Take this one, for instance, as surprising as it is clear. Maître Omraam Mikhaël Aïvanhov is speaking to young people: «You all know that in ancient times, the savages lit their fires by taking two branches and rubbing them together. The result was heat, because of the friction, the movement. If they continued rubbing the sticks together a flame appeared: light, fire! Why is it that everyone, young and old, know when they make love how to produce movement (friction) and heat (they must be hot since they remove their clothing), but they don't know how to produce light? Why do they stop at the level of movement, friction, heat, pleasure? What about the light? What about the divine side of love? They are not enlightened, something is escaping them, aren't they overlooking some-

---

* Volumes XIV and XV: «Love And Sexuality», Complete Works, Omraam Mikhaël Aïvanhov.

The Path Leading to the Rocher and the Sunrise

The Rock of Prayer

Sunrise at Le Bonfin

Saluting the Master – The Great Hall

The Great Hall – Interior

thing? Something that can be learned at an Initiatic and esoteric School: how to be enlightened and made divine by love, by the way we love.»

Again the Maître questions us: «Who is the inventor of religion?» This time the brothers have an answer. «It must be the Sun!» «Yes,» says the Maître. «The Sun invented religion.» We are still in the world of love, as you will see. «Heat is not what produces knowledge. It is the property of light to make us see things, light produces knowledge. The properties of heat are different. For instance, you can't be happy when you are frozen stiff. Cold stiffens us, makes us huddle up and shrink so as not to lose the little bit of heat we have left. And we are not joyful. With light, the mind dilates and opens up, it relaxes. Hence, when it is hot, not exaggeratedly so, of course... in the warmth, man feels the need to rejoice, to love, to be with others, because he is relaxed, he becomes expansive and wants to give. His joy and love inspire him with the desire to admire, to adore something, someone. And in this way, it is warmth that created religion. Take warmth away and religion will disappear. Warmth is the symbol of love: when you love someone, you feel warmly toward him; if you hate him, you are cold. When a girl falls in love, her heart is filled with warmth, she feels a great admiration, an adoration for her beloved... to her he is God, he represents God. That is religion. The girl is religious without, perhaps, having any religion! When you love money, when you adore it more than anything, that too is a form of religion... the religion of money... you may not believe in God, but you've got religion!»

And now, what is it that the life of the Sun brings us?

### 3. The World of life

The moment invariably comes for all collectivities when there are material problems that need to be solved. Our daily bread! Survival! And that is the common ground where men collide, where they lose their sense of brotherhood, where the materialist is lying in wait for the spiritualist: «But how will you manage?» We are entering the third of the three worlds at the School of Maître Omraam Mikhaël Aïvanhov, the level of the skin, the outside of the fruit.* The solar fruit: 1. the world of light forms the core, the kernel. 2. the world of warmth, love and religion forms the pulp of the fruit, with the juices of opposing currents.** 3. the periphery, the outer fruit, is where contact is made with the outside, where the money circulates. «How will we manage?» Well, the Master has the answer. He is not a spiritualist, he is not a materialist. He is practical, it is his power. I have never seen him act as a spiritualist with his head in the clouds, nor as a materialist with his head below ground. No. He is a pragmaticist. Meaning

* Author's note: This image of the solar fruit is not meant to be poetic, it is scientific information. One day this image will be pertinent to current events, so we remind you now, at the risk of being repetitious, that every organization or organism in the Universe, from the atom to the stars, can be visualized as a fruit, in three worlds: with the pit, the pulp and the skin; or a centre, a space and a periphery. Draw a circle with a compass and you will have this figure. From our brain to the Sun, from one of our cells to the Universe, everything fits into this image. The pit, the kernel, the centre, represents the world of light, that is where it all starts, that is what holds the information, the genetic code, the child. The meat is a matrix that expands, assures communications, emanates heat. The skin comes in contact with the outside, is the link with the biological, economic life. You will see at the end of this book that the solar fruit in three worlds can be found not only in the formal or functional side of people and things, but also in the movement of their history.

** Author's note: The nourishing currents that go from the pit to the outer skin, and the currents that go from the skin to the pit, so that the pulp will be alive, exactly like the blood circulating in our body.

that before he undertakes anything whatsoever, he wants to know how Nature resolves the problem. How does Nature resolve the economic problems of daily life, thermic, phototonic, energetic, etc... the problems of survival? «Ask the Sun,» he says. «He will give you the answer.» Everyone would like to know the answer... scientists, philosophers and political leaders. Here at the Initiatic School, the material problems are always settled, even the one of physical expansion going on actually to give the School breathing space. However dangerous the situation, in the end there is always a fraternal solution. That is the third miracle.

What does the Sun answer? It's very simple: the Sun lets life flow. That is all the Sun ever does, so that we will survive! And that is all the Master does. Like his solar model, he makes life flow for everyone, whoever they may be, whatever the misunderstandings. He is a model of someone who thinks only of making life flow. «If you make life flow, everything will fall into place, your health, your happiness, the entire economy of your body, and the body of the Brotherhood.»

And life flows. We begin our apprenticeship in economics at the Initiatic School in our daily tasks, constructing, working in the fields, workshops, kitchens, and in material organization... water, gas and electricity. We make life flow. The world of life is a great collective exercise, for one and all it is rugged work, you come out with more blisters on your hands than you have pride left in your head! Wonderful blisters, they brand us as workers for the future.

And we make life flow! At this School for advanced studies in higher economics and innocence, things become simple economically, they recover their original frankness, naturalness, and openness. Life and love are one and the same. You make life flow so that love will flow, the heart is the first consideration. You consider your brother. In a conflict you consider what will be advantageous for **him.** Yes, it is revolutionary. A new order of things, a new human order where economic problems stimulate love and act as leaven. The Master learned that from the Sun, he says, as he hands it on to us. Economy, not for the sake of war, but as a means of evolving toward brotherhood. Flowers do the same thing. Look at them in the fields, can't you see that they are more beautiful because they are together, in an economy that is not a means of asserting rights, but of radiating beauty, that has for goal not profit, but life together! What a lesson for all who are infatuated with the economy on the left or the economy on the right (or in my lady's belfry), not that their idea of mankind is not brotherly, they all use the word, but they all have the same dream, the impossible dream of brotherhood without any life flowing in it, like a child with no blood, or a plant with no sap. For them, brotherhood is the exploitation of the spiritual or material riches it affords, a façade brotherhood, without blood or sap. An impossible dream, for Europe or for the world. How can we expect to have brotherhood without the one thing that is brotherly, and with the things that separate us, the party, the possessions, the Market, the Mart.

Yes, here in France, in this ancient and intemperate country that blows hot and cold at the same time, destiny (it will be called historic destiny one day) is offering a solution. To all people in high places, Maître Omraam Mikhaël Aïvanhov is proffering his plan for a new world economy based on brotherhood. Beginning with moral brotherhood. We've never thought of that. We have another kind of morality, of the party, of ideas, of our gods which we use to glorify ourselves and attack others, but we have no morality of the heart, no brotherliness. Here the morality of brotherhood comes first. And as brotherhood is necessarily universal, our morality is also universal and Cosmic.* A real solar revolution! To-day in France, the Maître explains it to us. **He resolves the problems of our human economy with the laws of the Cosmic economy!** Not in an abstract, unrealizable way, nor with the hazy impractical philosophy prevalent to-day. No, this morality is lived, it is practical and structured. All his efforts, all his knowledge, all his love go into being the model of his idea. He makes the life of the Brotherhood flow the way the Sun makes the life of the Cosmos flow... and everyone has his fill. His daily bread.

Our daily bread... so simple: a little flour, a little clear water, a little salt and yeast, a drop of oil, a hot fire in the oven... so little, really. Why is it obtainable only through suffering and the sweat of the brow for some, and not obtainable at all for others in spite of the sweat of their brows? Why is it we are still mammalian, some of us stuffed to overflowing while others are empty and exhausted, with nothing happening to alleviate the situation... on the contrary. Those who say that the first thing we need in order to stay alive on earth is food, are right, nothing will ever take the place of a good fresh loaf of bread... providing all the world's children also have theirs and that we don't know that 500,000,000 of them have none... none today, none tomorrow, none ever. We see their anxious faces on television as we sit down to supper. And even if all the children in all the Initiatic schools donated their bread, how many would it satisfy? A few dozen, for a few hours. Question: whose fault is it? Answer: the psychosis of materialism. We have had proof. From our earliest days at school on up through our lives, that is what deadens the heart, robbing it of all simplicity and naturalness. Parents are always advising: «work hard!» but for the heart: nothing.

* Volume XII, «Cosmic Moral Laws», Complete Works, Omraam Mikhaël Aïvanhov.

Nothing to make love flow, as life flows. Nothing to make the idea of brotherhood circulate... how can you expect bread to circulate? Cause and effect! There is no such thing as chance. The materialistic sect (the worst of all sects) has plunged us into the current of tension and heart attacks, depression and negativism. We are ill from it. It is Dante's Inferno, it is a bottleneck that's becoming dangerously tight... no bread gets through! One grim day, nothing will circulate any more, neither money, nor words, everything will be blocked. And then, to remove the obstruction, they will have to release the atoms. The laser. So that life can flow.

«Let life flow,» says Maître Omraam Mikhaël Aïvanhov, «make sure that everything is kept open and that communications are unhindered, so that love can flow!» That is his Initiatic message to mankind as this century comes to an end. In olden times, it was a question of alerting a few isolated egocentrics, exhorting them to save their souls, telling them they were living in illusion and that they had best move on to something else. Each one sought communication with God separately and ate his bread in solitude without worrying about other people and their bread, which is still the way it is in India, and the young in search of folklore and evasion are attracted by it. They are confused about communication. That school has served its time, to-day everything has changed. The currents of Aquarius are opening up incredible ways of communication through sound and image, satellites and supersonics, rapidity and weightlessness... it's extraordinary! When we can go nearly as far as the Heart of God, what do we want with ashrams and monasteries? It seems silly to-day to try to save one's soul by penance and indulgences and prayers for the remission of sins, ungenerous to settle our Karma and our debt to God with sanctimonious hypocrisy. All that is obsolete. Now it is a question of saving mankind, of making certain that men's hearts survive. A question of bread. A question of letting ourselves be open, all of us together, to the sounds, the images, the satellites, the speed and the weightlessness. «Let life flow and love will flow!» says the Master, entrusting us with a sample of the most rapid means of communicating life and love: the Brotherhood!

**He makes us go through the world of light so that we will see the source of life: the Sun! he makes us go through the world of warmth so that we will see each other: through the Sun! he makes us go through the material and economic world so that we will learn to let love flow as life flows: from the Sun!**

I remember something. One day the Master assembled us in the great Hall and asked us to sing. Song is used here as a method of creating atmosphere. We all sat down here and there, without worrying about the usual separate grouping of sopranos, tenors, altos and basses. We pointed this out. «Stay where you are, and sing!» he replied. The songs, or hymns, are expressly composed by the late Master Peter Deunov to awaken the spiritual forces of the heart. We sing. Not being confined to any one group, each voice tends quite naturally to blend harmoniously with the voice next to it, not only to the part it belongs to. The result is amazing. Currents other than usual, an atmosphere other than usual. All the song's meaning is brought out, moving us to our depths. In the long silence that follows, we feel our joint emotion. The Maître says: «That is the way to sing.» He was speaking about the music, but he was also speaking about mankind, about the Brotherhood, about the future, gently pointing out (always gently) that a solar ambiance cannot be created with antiquated methods that only emphasize form, that the solar ambiance begins with the core, the heart, and that each one of us

must blend into the whole before trying to stand out ourselves, so that life can flow. Of course it isn't easy, the flowers
have an easier time than we do. The bad habits we acquire at
school accustom us to the opposite, to separate rows and separate groups and a leader for each one, precisely because his
voice sings solo while the rest raise their voices against him.
We are proud of being separate. It's the same everywhere, in
families, in society, in syndicates and politics. Each one has
his badge pinned to his lapel. His label. That's what we like.
«The Brotherhood, which is the expression of unity and not
of separation, can only exist,» said the Master that day, «if it
is a thing of the heart, only if we think about nothing else but
making life flow. Only then will the solar atmosphere spread
over the earth.»*

* Author's note: An example of Maître Omraam Mikhaël Aïvanhov's
methods. It would take volumes to describe all the methods he uses to correct the errors in our daily activities. There is more than singing. When we
are building a wall, or painting it, hammering a nail, planting a tree, gar-
dening, preparing vegetables, cooking, cutting a path through the brush,
opening a door, using a knife, slicing a watermelon, walking along the
road... etc. etc... for him everything is an opportunity to point out the real
meaning behind things, either by his own example, or by the explanation
and interpretation he gives us. I am witness to that. But this is what I wanted to say: his pedagogy, his teaching of how to «make life flow», is not
based on some vague friendly philosophy (let's all get together and be brotherly). No, there is nothing new in that. What makes his way new is that each
time, this Master brings everything back to the original solar structure, the
order you are beginning to be familiar with: Light, Love, Life (my theme,
the subject of this book). In this way he creates the solar atmosphere we are
so badly in need of; for «life to flow», we come to realize that we must begin with Light. And therefore, whether we are singing or forming a world
government (more on that later), everything must begin with the authority
of Light, with reflexion, with a meditation on the meaning of what you are
starting and what you can expect as a result, the effects and consequences of
your undertaking. And then everything must be warmed by Love, by feeling
in unison, singing in unison, legislating in unison, according to the authority of Light. And only afterwards, after the unity of Love is formed, come
the different methods, the diverse tendencies and temperaments that make
up the harmony. Today we have the bad habit of doing things in the opposite direction, we begin with division, particularity, prejudice. And life can't

In his desire to help us, there is nothing that he does not throw light on, from the art of singing, eating, breathing, working, loving, all the way to a good relationship with Nature spirits. The universality of the Teaching is surprising... I write this for those who, not knowing, might imagine that an Initiatic Teaching forces a way of thinking on you. The opposite is true. This Teaching helps us escape from the system we know: conventional, intellectual, restricted, sentimental, chaotic, materialistic, and narrow in outlook. We escape not only through our choice of model, unique, universal and solar, but through the multiplicity of methods available, through the language that is universal. You have no idea! I can only say that since I began to live the Teaching, I feel free, I am wonderfully liberated. The lack of universality in the world around us is appalling... the gestures one has to make, the courses one has to take, the way one must think and behave, the obligations one is compelled to accept, all the conforming we must do in order to earn our daily acceptance in society... how inhibiting, to say the least, for the heart! And how narrow the academic idea of man's happiness! Or the Church's idea. What a lack of universality, of catholicity in the etymological meaning of the word... it's demoralizing, the demoralizing life the young are asked to live. They let us know their reactions! The Master I am telling you about, opens up for us a Universe of liberty and space, and for it to be available to all, he offers a multiplicity of methods. It is a brand new cultural contribution, to me as important as the alphabet, printing press, radio, satellite, or any other means of communication which will one day be put to good use by the Universal Brotherhood. It is the language of Aquarius, which favours life and encourages it.

---

get through! I bow before the Master, I render homage to him for the model he gives us of his faith in the solar order (making us believe) and for his simplicity in applying it to daily living (giving us practice). It takes genius, as mankind will recognize one day, to create such a resurgence of life.

Up to now, we have been limited as to the application of human science. We were told that to be happy we must do and say certain things in a certain way, believe in certain dogmas (however antiquated), in sects for happiness, in opposition to one another and out of communication with each other. Prisons! Maître Omraam Mikhaël Aïvanhov helps us jump over the chalked line we draw around our hearts, hypnotizing ourselves into thinking it cannot be crossed! He launches the solar revolution by the multiplicity of his methods, which makes them universal, exactly as a solar ray offers a multiplicity of fruit, flowers and beauty to guarantee the biological survival of man, universally. One is staggered by the abundance of the works of this Master... is there in the history of man anyone who has left so many practical, easy, familiar, lovable and efficient things to go by? How can we measure such a Being? How can we even describe the tremendous knowledge of man and the Universe he has?

A language is universal when everyone is in resonance with it, when it makes everyone vibrate the same way. And if the genius of this Master gives us a number of methods for living our lives, our nights and days from dawn to sundown and on to dawn again, the universality of his methods permits us to select the one with which we are in tune. Otherwise there would be useless superabundance. Each season has its fruit, some are good when picked, some later. The Eucharistic ritual is good for some and not for others. We adapt our way of life to life itself and vary our language in the same way, depending on whether we are talking to one person or many, whether we are writing a book, a play, or a film. The words, the rhythm, the tone, change... to express the same truth. Even if it is not always the truth! The important thing is for life to flow through the language. There cannot possibly be a set way of talking about happiness, for instance. Atheists,

· Catholics, Jews, Arabs, Protestants, all have the same idea of happiness – the Sun – but no two believe the same way. Language becomes universal when it embraces all kinds of methods, so that no roads are blocked and life can flow. The important thing is that life be made to flow, and the language of Maître Omraam Mikhaël Aïvanhov makes life flow. Truly. I bear witness. He makes the solar truth appear credible to all men, all hearts and minds, whatever the colour, customs, or language, whatever the season or weather. A universal language, so that the Sun will rise and life will flow, in us. One day it will be used by new writers, new artists, new inventors, new philosophers, politicians, and pundits, newly disenchanted with materialism. They will know how to make life flow. It will be their craft, they will be the craftsmen. This Teaching is for the craftsmen of good will everywhere who want to work faithfully for the advent of Universal Brotherhood. For the Golden Age! The Age that will have the Sun as its model, the model whose methods are clearly presented to us each morning as it rises : Light, Love and Life, the methods of the universal University!

«O Sun, my Brother! As you appear on the horizon and rise into the sky in glory, may the Sun of LIGHT rise in my intelligence!»

«O Sun, my Brother! As you appear on the horizon and rise into the sky in glory, may the Sun of LOVE rise in my heart!»

«O Sun, my Brother! As you appear on the horizon and rise into the sky in glory, may the Sun of LIFE rise in my body!»

Do you know a more practical or effective prayer, corresponding more exactly to what our heart longs for: a single model and multiple methods? Gratifying the heart, for that is what it needs: a love unique as the Sun's love, as luminous, warming, and restoring, since without that the heart becomes confused, depressed, and lost... it dies (a clinical fact); and the vastness of infinity around it, without which it also dies (also a clinical fact). In short, the heart needs great space around a fixed central point, room for the imaginary around a permanent unchanging love. That is the heart's desire. But nowadays, it is the other way round, love is anything but permanent and the room allotted to the imaginary gets smaller and smaller. That is why the heart is dying. Maître Omraam Mikhaël Aïvanhov restores the heart by giving it the essential: an example of love, and space for the imagination: universal Brotherhood. Do we know enough to accept it?

«Let life flow!» says Maître Omraam Mikhaël Aïvanhov. He admitted to us one day that he knew nothing at all about politics, administration or economic science, and that he had a great admiration for people who knew how to organize, but that he, instead of learning all that, had concentrated on observing Nature and the Sun, from which he had learned one thing only: that wherever there was water flowing, there were also grass and flowers, birds, insects, animals... and human beings, who came and installed themselves... because of the water. And when there was no flowing water, if the spring ran dry, they all left, the humans, the animals, the birds, the flowers, and last of all, the trees. «The same thing happens inside man,» he went on, «when there is no flowing water (love) in him, people, animals, birds, insects, flowers and trees abandon him (this is symbolic, they stand for qualities and attributes, virtues, faculties, forces and riches he no longer has) and man becomes a desert. Millions of people are deserts because they are not informed. Their hearts are so bare and poverty-stricken that everyone and everything leaves them alone, they don't even know why. No one has ever told them these things. There are too many deserts in the world. Nothing is more important than to make the water flow. That is what the Sun does, it is all the Sun ever does, make life flow. Life, water, love, are all the same thing... in different domains.»

I started out by saying that this Master's first concern was for the atmosphere, the ambiance of his Brotherhood.* We see why: so that water will flow! Water, when it is allowed to

---

* Author's note: Actual witnesses are the only ones in a position to say that the Master begins with the ambiance, for ambiance is not something you can tell about, it has to be lived. Something is «ambiant» that encompasses, envelops, pervades, as air and music are ambient. Ambiance is an etheric force. The ambiance created by a person then, is the ensemble, the aggregate of all the forces that vibrate, emanate, and radiate from him: his aura. When I say that this Master begins by the ambiance, I mean that he is himself ambient in that he vibrates, emanates, and radiates as the solar model. That is what I mean by the ambiance being his first concern, his constant vigilance, as he puts currents into circulation, the forces of light, love, and life. To have a better idea of this Initiatic Teaching about which we know so little, practically nothing, we must bear in mind the double aspect of the solar order of the Universe: the descending current (light, warmth and life = movement), and the ascending current (life, warmth and light). The Master manipulates the two currents according to the situation and the people involved, on whether he is acting on the spiritual or the material level, on what forces he wants to release. Inspired and practical. And he invites us to create ourselves this ambiance as a preliminary to the unimpeded circulation of life. In this way, there is nothing cold or rigid or incidental about his Teaching. It is natural and joyful. Is there a single educator on his podium who is concerned with solar ambiance, still less with being a solar example? The solar ambiance corresponds exactly with the needs of the brain and the conditions of its development. Our brain is the prolongation of the senses, and has, therefore, the same character as our senses. It needs information that is sensible, not abstract, it needs information as to the biological milieu in which it lives, which formed it: it needs the Sun. Globally! The brain dislikes prejudice, the «party», partitions, division, eye-wash and bluff. It is distressed by these things, and distress leads to violence. Ask the students! Truly, the Initiatic methods of education presented by the Master are something entirely different.

flow, organizes everything, you can see it; water (with no schooling, no diplomas), knows exactly how to arrange things so they work properly! That is why the Master never bothers with organization; if the water flows, organization takes care of itself. His School, his Brotherhood, is the example, the proof, of what I am saying and it's marvellous to see. How many fabulous organizations are there in the world, where every detail is carefully planned and executed and nothing is missing... except water (water is invariably forgotten), and in a little while, because water (love) is missing, the whole organization collapses... too much calculating and not enough water! Or take an electric installation... the equipment, the machinery is all there, but nothing works because someone forgot to turn on the current! How often do political movements hold meetings, congresses, seminars, symposiums, reunions, to announce at last their common programme? Alas! Nothing works, no one turned on the water, everyone forgot that you have to begin with love. It is a solar revolution, to start with love. A solar revolution, since as we know, the Sun starts out by making life flow. Love and life are one and the same.

As I witness this stupendous turning in history, I often ask myself what it was that prompted the Master to make the water flow. As you know, the symbol of Aquarius shows an ancient Sage pouring water out of an urn. Here is the question; I leave the answer to you: why was this Master born under the constellation of Aquarius, with four planets including the Sun and the Moon in conjunction with Aquarius? Why was he born in 1900 at precisely the time when the world was just coming under the influence of Aquarius?

However, dear reader, I have not yet mentioned the most important thing concerning this world of life and economics, I haven't told you the essential, the rarest, hardest thing to find in the world, the only thing that permits you to judge the elevation of someone's mind correctly, to know whether he is a real Initiate, a Master, or not. I tell it to you now, to-day, when mass ignorance prevails to such a surprising degree: people think it normal for an instructor, an «Initiate», to accept money, to be paid for his teaching, without ever wondering where he comes from or what he has in his head, what his ideals are and what his goal... the masses are naïve, a few titles (bestowed on himself by himself) are enough for them: he has qualifications, let him open a school! We've seen this and we are going to see more and more of it. «Initiates» exploit the public today without bringing them anything good, luminous or salutary; Indians, Hindus, Sadhus, so-called, Maharadjas, all are paid. No Hindu sage would have considered such a thing in the past. Are they influenced by Americans, to be so money-minded? A shame, a disgrace for the great Hindu philosophy. Human beings are so lacking in judgment that they deserve to be cheated; when confronted with a real teacher who works gratuitously, they distrust him, they treat him like a pick-pocket. «It's not normal!» they say. It so happens that Maître Omraam Mikhaël Aïvanhov has been working for forty-two years without pay! It's true. The land he bought near Fréjus, years ago, for three thousand old Francs (now worth several hundreds of thousands of new Francs), he gave to the Brotherhood. To-day it is the Bonfin. He has given everything to the Brotherhood. To find out whether someone is sincere and honest, you have to look at his motives and see whether they are selfish or not, isn't that so? The Master is completely disinterested. His big secret is that he never asks for money. From anyone. Yet in spite of all his generosity, his light, the world has poured spite and malice on him, beginning with the newspapers which have accused him of ridiculous things... lies, nonsense, downright wickedness. I have read it all, and I would call it terrible if it were not such blasphemy (I've also read somewhere that the Master's eyes are blue. At least I know what colour they are : not blue.) The great wide public which never verifies anything they read, believes it all. Journalists are not stupid, they know what to write in order to make their papers sell ; people revel in horror stories, crime, scandal, pornography. They are unaccustomed to hearing sublime, heavenly things because they are surrounded with the exact opposite, and when they read something negative, something inhuman, they believe it instantly because that is what they're used to, they are like that themselves. I am aware, as I write about the glorious and wonderful things I have lived and learned during my life with the Master, that I will be accused of being hypnotized, out of my mind, bewitched, of selling out to a dubious cause, of being involved in shady business. But actually, who is bewitched, the Initiates who come to us with their light, or human beings who live in the dark? I write with sadness that if the Master had **not** brought his light, had not tried to enlighten mankind and to extricate us from our negative materialism, he would never have been attacked. «Poor humanity!» sighs the Master upon occasion. How heartfelt and how revealing.

The thing that I wanted to say, and it will surprise you, is that this Master finds it perfectly normal and natural to be attacked in this way. This proves for me that he is an Alchemist: he takes the stones that are thrown at him and transforms them into precious stones, thus growing ever stronger and stronger. He keeps evolving toward perfection.

This extraordinary resourcefulness of the heart is what we will now go into.

Exercise Area

The Exercises

# THE INITIATIC AND ESOTERIC SCHOOL
# OF
# MAITRE OMRAAM MIKHAEL AIVANHOV

## *THIRDLY, THE MEANING:*
## *The way to Brotherhood*

## A MASTER EVOLVES... TOWARD PERFECTION

In the future, when the children of the XXIst Century read in their history books about the Initiatic and Esoteric School of Maître Omraam Mikhaël Aïvanhov, they will see that the worlds of Light, Love, and Life, the three worlds that we were taught to live in our hearts, were each one represented symbolically, by three different localities, three High Places. The Rock of Prayer represents the world of Light, the culminating point, the centre, where the auric vibrations, as the Master once told us, are the same as on the peaks of the Himalayas. The great Hall, the physical centre of the School represents the world of Love (warmth) where we hear the Word... where the lectures are held, where the recording studios, offices, and kitchens are, and just outside, the exercise area and the circle for the Fire at Michaelmas. The rest of the Camp, the different accomodations and installations, the work areas, the tracts of land, the vineyards, herb and kitchen gardens, the greenhouses, the orchards... is the world of Life. This form is the model of the future society that the Master will leave the world, scientists and scholars, philosophers and politicians. But what I want to tell you is this: the Master appears to us (and we to him) in a different way in each place. On the Prayer Rock, he is the Prophet, he is Ram, he is Moses, he is Jesus, and we are his followers. In the Hall, we prepare for his coming, we meditate to create the right ambiance, inviting him to come, he accepts if he wishes, and there, he is the Initiate, our Teacher. Outside, in the world of work, the work of the collectivity which we more or less organize ourselves, the Master comes to see us as a father... in white, white hat and stick in hand, a father who gives advice and comfort. All that I have seen to date, everything I know about this Master, everything he does, convinces me that he relives in his heart the same bitter disappointment as Moses... and Jesus... (neither the love of the Father nor the wisdom and knowledge of the Initiates are enough to save mankind)... which gives me a glimpse of what will happen here at this School. Soon we will be shown only the Prophet on the Rock of Prayer. And when the time has come for history to unfold and the new millenium to begin, this Master will appear before all men of good will, an Image, as on the Sinaï heights, as on the Mount of Olives, as at Golgotha, an Image of the Sun at its height. The image of a new mankind.

And so, staggering as it will be for the men of the new era of the Sun to contemplate this image, icon in hand, they will not be experiencing the essential. To see the live image is the essential: the solar Being who lives in our time, now, the oasis we reached during the long trek across the desert when we were at our thirstiest, the essential, is here and now. To meet a living Master is a privilege without equal. A living Master is no image, he is not standing motionless in the sky of history with his feet on a pink cloud. He is alive! He breathes! We feel his breath and sense his fragrance, we see the sweat on his brow. Alive, he acts out for us the drama of the Initiatic Life, showing us the movement of his own solar life, how he traces with his heart the stars and the revolving seasons. Life is movement, that is its great virtue, it follows its course in time and space, in a solar trajectory across the stars and the zodiacal periods: evolving! This Master also pursues his evolution, this is what I am trying to say. He evolves! There in front of us, here and now! His life spirals upward to the Sun and he becomes more and more like a Sun himself in his soul, in his consciousness and in his body, as everyone can see. Using the words that have always expressed these things flatly and simply: he becomes magnified before our eyes as he gives himself for us. That is the essential, no one can give more. No image, neither the image of Jesus, nor the image of Moses, can ever give as much. Two thousand years, four thousand years, have gone by.

As I write, I realize that I am living the most extraordinary thing that a man could wish for: to be a witness to to-day. It's clear: I am watching a Being evolve and be magnified a thousand billion times faster than all the people we see on television put together, the learned, the philosophers, the politicians. Evolving because of the solar impetus he gives each one of his thousand million cells. It is true for us as well, but because he is in constant control, participating consciously and intelligently, he advances more quickly. And further. It makes one dizzy to think of it. In short, I have seen a higher Being in the process of evolving, continuing his evolutive progress in the solar system, moving always nearer to the Sun, acquiring the same qualities, thinking of nothing else. He is the Sun's corolla, or the point of florescence. That is the word! And the Sun's aura fills him with virtue, reflected in his smile, his skin, his look, his voice, and in the movement of his hands, like... yes, like the corolla of a flower in bloom.

This a where the story becomes history. Memorable, told and retold by the children of the XXIst Century who will know it by heart. They will know about evolution and talk about it among themselves.

## *EVOLUTION TOWARD PERFECTION:*
### *The Way of Hope*

Evolution toward perfection is the subject of this book. The dictionary says that evolution is a series of progressive transformations in the same direction for the improvement in quality of a living species. Remember the words, transformation, direction, improvement, quality. Words of hope! Why did neither Carl Linné, who etablished fundamental bases for classifying the species, nor Charles Darwin, who later added the evolutive movement or struggle for existence, nor Jean Rostand, who wrote not very long ago that the human species was the **end** of a long series of evolutive transformations... why is it that none of them (and probably no one else) ever had the idea or the occasion to observe one of his fellow human beings, a man, from the point of view of the evolution of the heart, in order to grasp what the progressive transformations would be, in which direction they would be moving, and what would be the qualities they would be gaining. Still less did anyone think of contemplating an Initiate. Had they done so, they would have understood the limitation and error of their thinking. In their over-concentration on animals, they overlooked the fact that man also was committed to a gradual evolution in the solar system, that even an Initiate is a link in the evolutive succession of the species, a door opening upon other still more evolved Cosmic beings. *The existence of the Initiate proves that swifter, more powerful and luminous beings exist, beings who may be beyond our slow comprehension but who are conceivable in an infinity of space that is ceaselessly evolving.* For everything evolves ceaselessly in time and space, rocks and stones, plants, animals and men, and also whatever exists above and beyond us. Everything evolves toward the Sun in order to acquire life, love and light. Everything has that hope; you have it also, although you don't know it. The whole solar system itself is in the process of evolving in the direction of the constellation of Hercules. Toward other qualities. It is the kinematic dream of celestial space, spaces of hope. Therefore, why not hope in a God* who can be approached through a series of transformations, out of common sense, out of the desire to have the same qualities, His qualities.

On the subject of evolution and the hope it offers, Maître Omraam Mikhaël Aïvanhov says the following: «Evolution is significant if it means to become perfect, if it is evolution toward perfection. When you participate consciously in your own evolution, with your will, your love, and your mind, then evolution is something unique and divine. In any case, everything evolves, only the change is imperceptible. Biologists consider it an impulse of Nature that propels creatures forward, but so slowly that it takes thousands and thousands of years to get anywhere. Why hasn't evolution given us the Kingdom of God on earth? Because it is a vegetative process in which human beings do not participate, are not willing to participate. Only Initiates evolve swiftly and surely, coming close to perfection in a single incarnation. That is missing in ordinary human beings. Of course in recent years with all the inventions and discoveries, evolution has been accelerated, but it is not yet perfection. Perfection is something else, it touches other realms. Cosmic Intelligence has put an atom in every one of his creatures, enabling each one to become per-

* Author's note: The word «God» was created by the Initiates themselves, who used the form, the meaning and the contents of the Chaldean alphabet to disclose the genesis and the organization of the Universe that scholars are only just beginning to explore. The Kabbala sheds light on the meaning of the word: God. Many explanations can also be found in the Works of Maître Omraam Mikhaël Aïvanhov. God: a word to explain the anatomy, the physiology and the psychology of the Universe. God, indicating the movement needed in order for life to exist and the life needed in order for movement to exist... to us a mystery.

fect as his Heavenly Father is perfect... but it takes millions and billions of years. If one were conscious of the results to be obtained, if one were enlightened, if one worked on this atom, there could be tremendous results. In India there are fakirs, yogis, who show you the seed of a fruit, a mango for instance, and a few hours later, the fruit will appear, ripe and ready to eat. Proof that perfection can be obtained quickly! Human beings don't realize that it is possible to obtain results in very little time, providing you know how to apply the white magic of concentration and imagination. We all have an image of perfection within us, but when it is not nourished, it develops very slowly. Yogis, the Saddhus, know about the force called Akasha; it is what they use to accelerate the maturation of the fruit or plant...»

The Master said these words to me quite recently, words of hope, delivering us from evil. I pass them on to you.


## EVOLUTION TOWARD PERFECTION:
### The Way of Power

One day I was working at something when the Master passed by. I had been going through a series of dramatic events, upsetting enough to require constant control to hold back the tears. I thought I had succeeded, no doubt not entirely, for he took me by the elbow: «This is no time to break down», he said. I may not have understood on the spot, but now I know what he meant: to be affirmative, to be as positive and affirmative as the Sun. It is his power, it is all he thinks about, all he does... affirm the Sun in his inner life, in his heart. The Sun never makes a shadow and neither does the Master. In the most dire circumstances, I have never seen him be other than affirmative, positive as the Sun. He acts as though he were the Sun, as though he was being watched the way we watch the Sun. He presents our eyes and hearts with a solar spectacle. A model of power and strength! Jesus said: «We are the sons of God.» Moses said: «Ye are Gods.» The Initiate I am describing lives that way, there before our eyes. He plays his part, the exacting role of solar performer in the tragi-comedy of the Cosmos. He submits, he plays his role. He has the knowledge, the will, the power, the audacity, and he is silent. If ever I dared ask him, he would say that he would like to play his part like a god, I'm certain. He is a solar magus.

The false ideas we have been taught, the ideas we learn in the catechisms of our Judeo-Christian religion are swept aside in one stroke. The Inquisition we were put through; the shadows we were held back in; the Hell we were committed to for our faults and our mortal sins, our apostasies, heresies, sorceries; the weight we bore as «miserable sinners», our backs bent under every kind of misery... have left us emasculated, complexed, neurotic, psychotic (Judeo-Christian psychosis) and faced with the rising tide of violence, the rising black tide of oil-slick. An exaggerated picture? It is the naked truth we see every day on television... shadows, darkness, tragedy, subterranean experiences according to Freud (not the example to follow). No place here for light or virtue, for heroes or heroism, for knights in armour, for Masters, or for holy joy. Our minds are blocked, we are impotent and helpless, while the Initiate continues to move toward the Sun. He demonstrates the difference! He starts out as we do with the same need for water, air and light. Like us, he is subject to conflicts, to opposition, he evolves because of opposition, because of his two opposing natures (like us). He feels pleasure and displeasure as we do, he has a taste for certain things and not for others, and like us, he is constantly coming up against people who are caught in their own oppositions, motivated by the lower currents of greed and jealousy and aggressivity and fear and self-defence and doubt. He lives both his violence and our violence. And in spite of that he never stops emanating, radiating, shining like the Sun, and like the Sun, is always trying to enlighten, to warm, to enliven, to bring us to flower. It's astounding, impossible, unimaginable... almost. Try it and see. He is always moving in the direction of evolution, of perfectionment. That is his power, his magic, to affirm the solar process, the improvement, the flowering, the magnificence without interruption. Never doubting, but always, as we said, always under the most difficult conditions.

Vanity, vanity, you say. Very well, let's take this word vanity... from the Latin, vanus, meaning void. A void? Vanity that elates, a void? A power would be more exact. When I see this Being who has taken the Sun as his model, who admits he is magnified by the Sun... if it is vanity that he has, then vanity is a glorious power, a divine power. Moses coming back down Mount Sinaï. Jesus thrashing the Pharisees and Sadducees and the existing establishment, wasn't it divine power they needed (and were receiving)? In their minds, no confusion with pride, pride wants to do without God. No, on the contrary. Their pride depended on God completely, it was not empty for it was filled with Him, and it was a natural power, because Nature abhors a void. If you have the power that fills you with life (you need it in order to survive), if this power illuminates your consciousness, warms your heart, stimulates you and fills you to overflowing with good health (as it does the Initiate), are you going to deny it? Vanity if you like, but isn't vanity more a question of fuzzy imagery, more in tune with our blurred ideas of the future, void of sense and meaning, void of God, but full of the human and personal conceit that causes all our distress? The Master I am talking about has a celestial, Cosmic vanity that fills his heart, quite obviously. He evolves, he perfects himself, he wants to become like his Heavenly Father, as Jesus told us to do : «Be ye perfect as your Father in Heaven is perfect». Call it what you will but this power is capable of making life divine, of accelerating your qualities, of transforming void into plenty... Vanity? Or the movement of survival of the heart, since it fills the heart with Sun. Vanity is part of the evolution toward perfection... but call it anything you like, that is not the important thing. The important thing is that all this exists and fills us with hope, power, life, warmth, and the light that permits us to be happy and healthy, and brothers, and together. And so, if we are magnified because of it, let us be grateful for its existence.

## EVOLUTION TOWARD PERFECTION:
### The Only Way to Solve the Problem of Survival in a Brotherly Way

Every day on television we are told that the economic contingency is critical and that all our difficulties stem from there. We accept, we actually believe that our troubles come from that, we repeat it to each other until it becomes an obsession, so impressed are we by the gravity of our leaders, the learned, the philosophic, and the political. Well, the Initiatic School is here to give the lie to all that, and to teach us something else : that it is the overall contingency of ignorance, our ignorance, that is responsible for all our trouble. This may seem surprising, but if you think about it you will see that by choosing to remain ignorant about the movement of life toward perfection, we created a barrier, we have blocked things. And it is because everything is blocked that we repeat the words of despair and impotence : the overall economic contingency is critical... as if one day it would be less critical... and we think about this, about when life will be easier. It is a misconception, it means that we in our ignorance, are being led astray. And it means we don't observe things that happen to us... in life... for it is plain that man is less troubled by the economy itself than by the incessant fluctuation of the economy, which forces him to be continually readapting himself. A sign that there is life behind it, a live, intelligent plan, but unknown, nameless and incomprehensible to man.

We have a name for it at the Initiatic School. It is called the movement of evolution toward perfection. It sustains all things, and keeps everything in motion. It is the cosmic event we live by, universal and common to all. That is the contingency! If you add the flowers, birds, butterflies and trees around your house, you will see that this is true. The contingency is the ocean of life, our plasmatic and sanguineous ocean, our cellular and stellar and solar ocean: the rolling waves of history. The cause of our survival together in brotherhood despite ourselves.

In the ocean of life (the contingency) there are three currents with which you are now familiar: the current of light, the current of warmth or love, the current of life! They flow, making it possible for us to quench our thirst for those three things that are indispensable to us. Here and now, in our bodies, we are plunged into the current of warmth in our hearts, into the current of light in our minds. This is no abstraction, it is our daily life, and whether we wish it or not, we cannot escape. We can only recognize that it is so. From morning on, we are involved and influenced, first by the current of life in which our bodies wake up obligatorily, perhaps happily... but how to survive? With bread and with the daily sweat of our brow, of course. Then the current of warmth, on the street, in the crowd of brothers, our hearts laid bare, searching for a soul mate, for warmth in the early morning chill; it is the current of our sympathies and our antipathies, our secret sensuality, our sexuality. And lastly, our steps take us to our place of work, as they say. There our minds organize our work, for workers we are and always will be. Reflexion. Light.

Because of the Cosmic contingency, we are faced each morning with three questions:

How to live? (Life, the economy)

How to love and be loved? (Warmth, love, sexuality)

How to live in society? (Light and the politics of living together)

And for flowers, it is the same thing. They are in the same Cosmic ocean (the contingency), they have the same triple problem of survival: self-preservation, self-reproduction, self-control, or (you've guessed it), the economy, love and sex, politics. The difference being that flowers never forget the forward movement of evolution, they are not confused by words but obey the spirit, the life within. No complications for them! They live their history by evolving: vibrating, emanating, radiating fragrance, colour and health. They blossom, while we cut ourselves off from the inner life, we stop evolving, our evolution is blocked because of a few words: how to survive, how to love, how to live in society according to the rules. Pebbles! Pebbles barring the way. Economics, love, politics, are an impediment, and so we stand still while the flowers move steadily ahead toward their florescence.

«Let life flow», says the Initiate. Precisely: by economics, love, politics. Let them play their role! Through them, life can flow from Heaven into our fraternal body, three functions that make a living whole. It is mathematical, it is biological, it is Initiatic.

The chart opposite, drawn from what I learned at the Initiatic School, traces the way of evolution. Nowhere else is this taught: usually we learn about money, sex, the party (which is the goal of economics, love and politics... but only if we are content with the shape of the nose and forget about breathing). To be sure, we listen to marvellous speeches, full of emotion and oratory, but inside there is nothing, certainly not the idea of solar evolution, which is why everything is jammed. Progress is arrested because we take money, sex, and the party for the conclusion, the end. And the result is inevitably a war... the Hundred Year War, the thousand year war, religious wars, family wars, war between brothers, war between friends, war in History Books, war in our personal story-books, war in societies and fraternities (hypocritical to boot), war everywhere, war between everyone, war for the end of our noses and not the breath within, war for money, sex, and the party. War, the answer to our need for violence! At the University of Nanterre, they study the motivations behind group living. They should look for the answer on Mount Sinaï, nothing could be clearer. The group, with its money, sex and prejudice and the Initiate who held the crowd together in the desert with grandiose descriptions of the Promised Land: one day without him and it's all over. Abandon! Celebrate! The Golden Calf! Money! Sex! The Party! Violence! Assassinate the President! Crucify an Initiate! Pharisees and Sadducees, the police, the polyvalent, the interrogators: was it for money? Sex? The party? Our will for violence condemns on the grounds of fraud, or lewdness, or spying, while the crowd cheers (we are the crowd) and no one cares about the genius of the Initiate, or which Cosmic order he belongs to... or about you, Mr. President; those are the things that won your election for you... and those things will defeat you.

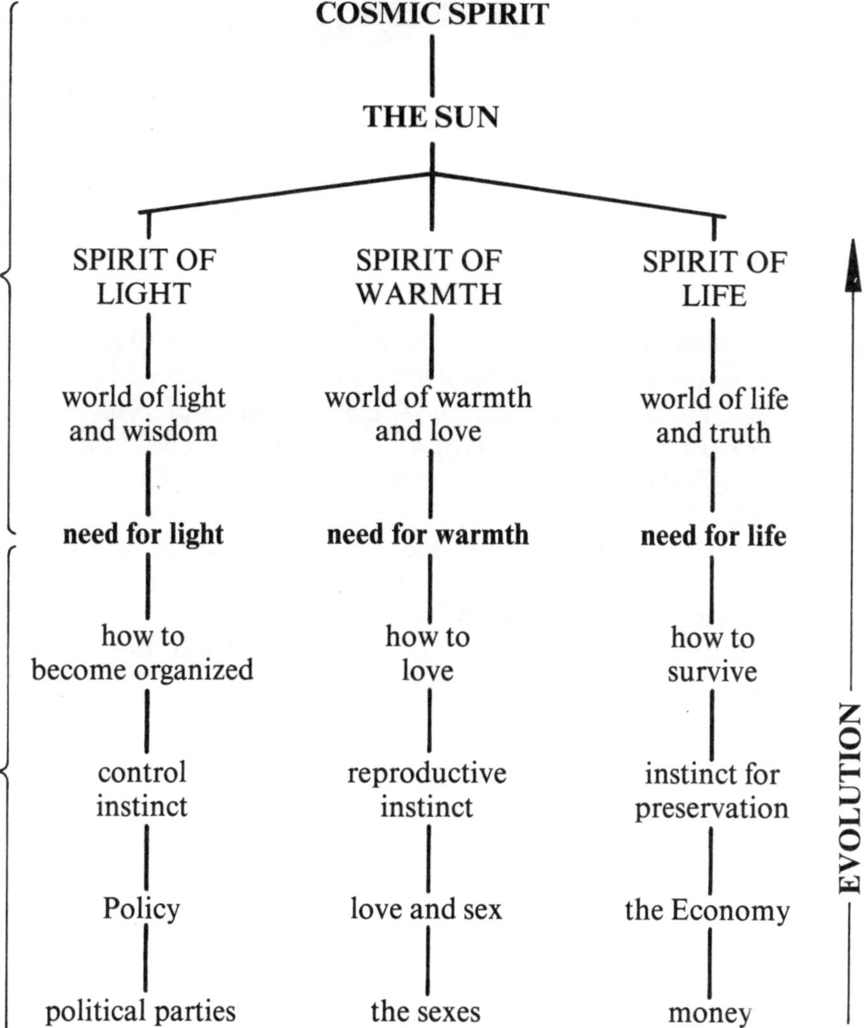

COSMIC SPIRIT

THE SUN

SPIRIT OF
LIGHT

SPIRIT OF
WARMTH

SPIRIT OF
LIFE

world of light
and wisdom

world of warmth
and love

world of life
and truth

need for light

need for warmth

need for life

how to
become organized

how to
love

how to
survive

control
instinct

reproductive
instinct

instinct for
preservation

Policy

love and sex

the Economy

political parties

the sexes

money

EVOLUTION

*Nothing happens without a reason; everything is «caused.» This drawing of our Cosmic and universal «contingency» shows the way in which our material problems of survival are linked to spiritual «causes». Any civilization that takes into consideration nothing but the material, is cutting itself off from its spiritual essence... thus accelerating the phenomenon of entropy and entering into decadence and decay, like all matter in the process of mortification.*

***The solar revolution*** *is the return of consciousness toward the principles of life. That is the* **quality of life** *to which the new man is committed. Today. Now.*

We talk about violence, we ask ourselves in the most bourgeois way where it came from, why we have it... and so I wonder, has any member of Government ever attended an Initiatic School? It seems there is only one thing that counts as far as the Government is concerned: money, to have money and make money. Turn on television: money! Could it be that our Government underestimates certain values that are the basis, the sine qua non for prosperity and for the glory of a country? The Government is not interested in the fact that there might be people trying to work for the good of the country, trying to create fine citizens, trying to purify the atmosphere, trying to heal the ill, do something permanently helpful with addicts, for instance... not interested, unimportant. What is important is how much money there is in the Treasury. Proving that those who govern haven't the slightest knowledge of human nature, and in the end, because of their ignorance, are criminally responsible for mobs, for thieves and for terrorists playing with bombs and explosives. Violence? Soon no member of any Government will be safe. One wonders why our leaders are not a little more clairvoyant. It would help them to see that there exist honest people who are perplexed about their Government, who wonder why there is never any mention of their effort and sacrifice, never any mention of goodness and kindness, generosity, integrity... yet they exist! What is more, they, the honest ones, are the ones who find themselves virtually strangled, their ideas and help refused everywhere; they feel desperately unhappy at being considered so useless. The heart of the people thinks that way to-day, ask the tradespeople, the «little» people, they will tell you that crime is the result of the fact that any one who is good and honest is jeered at, while those who are tricky, scheming, or simply dishonest are not only tolerated but rewarded.

And the Universal White Brotherhood receives this treatment. No one has ever come to verify whether the Brotherhood might not be doing something good for society and for the country, no, we are misrepresented, smeared, torn apart by the press in every possible way, newspapers, radio, books. Even tax collectors are out to do us in! No one can complain if criminals are becoming more and more numerous in the world.

Money, sex, politics! Our violent wills compel others to do our wills with such violence, it will destroy us all, life will be intolerable, life itself won't be able to stand it, it will explode like an atom... already it finds it difficult to survive. Life needs to breathe, to recover its forward movement, to resume its role and continue on its way, the way of evolution. Life is trapped! It will burst out of a sudden, breaking loose with a scream that will shatter our thick heads, penetrate our hearts and nerves, and cause disease, depression, dementia... and death, for once liberated, it will throw us into World War III, and we will die side by side in the ruins of our cities. If you don't believe it, ask someone to put in cartoon form for you the recent facts of history, such as the death trains headed for Auschwitz, the trenches filled with death at Verdun, the six hundred million children facing death to-day because of us (we can only spare them 5 percent of the world's total supply of food)*, our wilful violence! Turn the page and look at **your** children swollen with hunger, at trenches filled with fear, at prisons filled with you and me and the others, look at Hiroshima, for those who lived through it, it meant being alive in Hell. Next time it will be worse. There will not be more than a few thousand left to sweep up the dust in the four corners of the earth, according to the Scriptures. Through our fault. The

* 1979 figures.

fault of the economic contingency, the contingency of our ignorance, the stupid desire to reduce all social and human
problems to an economic level. The contingency of our materialistic, intransigent wills, which are all we have to lean on,
our only basis, our only information, our only entertainment,
the only message our party leaders send us, our love song, our
dream. But life is movement! Life is the inner evolution of
the spirit! And it will recover, for sure. The violence of three
or four billion wills is a lot of violence : life must be planning
a total explosion in order to begin again. You can feel it. Sing-
ers yell it to us to the accompaniment of electric guitars, yell
it to the world drowning in the rising tide of fear... 1980. And
then...

And then there is the Initiate. The model! Evolving, becoming perfect before our eyes, acting out his role of solar
mage, reflecting the shining power and the firm hope so necessary, so indispensable to-day. Power to found a Brotherhood based on the solar model. Power to enable the great currents of life to circulate from Heaven down to earth and back
again, and power to restore economics, love, and politics to
their true, rightful and glorious roles. Words of survival that
explain with great clarity and care what it is possible to do
and what it is not possible to do if we want brotherhood to exist on earth.

In the realm of the possible there is the evolutive movement toward perfection. That is the message of this Master. If
the word brotherhood means the link, the blood ties between
the members of a family, then the function, the role of these
ties, is to make life flow, to make the life of the Sun flow between the brothers so that each one can evolve toward his
own perfection. Brotherhood is a means of survival, Cosmic
survival, in the same way that thinking, breathing, eating are
means of survival. That is what we do at this School, meditate

together, breathe together, and eat our meals together. One could do it alone. However, the fact of doing these things together creates certain advantages that we are not yet aware of: the tremendous spiritual advantages of brotherhood.

Men think of the word brotherhood as denoting something pleasant, promising a permanent state of ease and comfort, which is what they are ready to settle for (it is all they want). That is what turns the word into something hard and cold like a pebble on the path, blocking the way, and it all begins again, with brothers behind guns shooting at other brothers behind guns. War. Look at history. Terrifying to think that brotherhood dies at the hand of brothers. In your history book it says, Liberty, Equality, Fratenity (at the time they meant it). But take another look at those barricades and the milling people, imagine it is your blood pouring into the Seine, turning the water red all the way to the Champ de Mars! Things would be different now, they sang as they danced the Carmagnole and cheered to the sound of cannon. The Revolution came and went. We thought we were going to «... love one another as I have loved you...», but nothing changed, nothing is better. On the contrary. Where is it leading, to what final terminal conflict? Against whom, dear God, since we are all brothers? We who made the Revolution and would make another one to-day, for the left or the right; we who try everything, common markets, policies, new policies, more policies, we who appreciate togetherness enough to make love on the Place de la Concorde, on the site of the gallows and the guillotine... we who quite sincerely don't believe in the Brotherhood of Man (the economic contingency makes it so difficult)... How many of us have died (loyal to the end) for nothing, because we never found out what was possible and what was not possible?

The **impossible** is all that is fixed and rigid. As, when we breathe, it is clear that the end of our noses is not what keeps us alive, but the life that flows into us through the nasal passages. It isn't the word brother, but the life that flows in the Brotherhood that makes it brotherly; not the economy, but the evolutive life within. It isn't you, my brother, but the life that flows from your heart to mine, uniting our hearts; not us, but love. The **impossible** is fixation. I write as I meditate, hoping to derive some comfort from the idea that there is something **possible** in spite of all that is impossible.

The **possible** is the movement of evolution toward inner perfection. I write this for you, my brother, to prepare your heart for the collective and fraternal life of Aquarius which will be ours in less than ten years: the **possible** is the evolutive movement within. I write for you, my friends, who have rejected the idea, because of your erroneous concept of the Brotherhood. I write it so that never again will we think it possible for brotherhood to exist side by side with the gallows, the scaffold, the cross, with prisons, military uniforms and other absurdities; even with common programmes and common markets, oil wells and rationed energy, with accountants and auditors of easy virtue or no virtue at all, with the desire for bread for oneself (and wine)... all that is impossible. All fixity is impossible. Nothing is rigid or permanent in Nature, nothing on earth is fixed except the «movement of inner evolution», every day, every night, from one season to the next. Nothing will ever be fixed except that movement. Life is movement! All the rest is function, in which each one plays his role. That is the truth, historically and cosmically.

If there is a revolution beginning in the world to-day, if a new society is forming which will go from industrial to scientific and finally to solar, we must not forget the movement of evolution toward perfection within. If we know that the problems to come will be geopolitical problems, solved by men who are still paleolithic (if not by data-processing centres), we still must not forget the evolutive movement of the life within.

The planet will follow its course, its project of industrialization, communication and information, all of which must not make us forget the movement of evolution toward inner spiritual perfection... no, all these coined words, cybernetics, electronics, cacophonics, must not be allowed to distract us from reality, «the evolutive movement toward inner spiritualization», the gradual ascent toward the florescence that will shatter our misconceptions and bring balm to our hearts.

This is what I believe, because I have lived it at the Initiatic and Esoteric School of the Great Universal White Brotherhood, where one draws on the «movement of the inner life» exactly as one draws on the air for breath, where life is good, my brother. Hearts and words are immersed in the same movement, and then, O Miracle! Everything becomes unblocked, including the economic contingency. It's true! One takes hold of the economy, delivering it from evil and plunging it into the living waters where it becomes innocent again, as in the beginning, innocent and naïve and at the same time revolutionary: economy, a function of survival of the Cosmos. There it is. The economy is no longer a question of frigidaires and vacuum cleaners, but of its own essence as a function of survival like a lot of other functions, my brother, like meditation, contemplation, identification, respiration, nutrition, procreation, imagination. A function that has existed since the beginning of time and always will exist, to ensure the production and distribution of Cosmic life. A function of man's evolution which is actually love, that is the way it will one day be understood, my brother. In a real democracy love belongs to the entire collectivity, love is the gauge of each one's aristocracy and nobility. And it works, life is good.

I have watched the brothers and sisters live in this movement of the heart. They are not dreamers, they are realists, solar artisans, men and women, craftsmen, colleagues, a family sharing the fresh hot bread baked in the early morning, sharing the fruit of their virtues and qualities so that each may take what he needs in the way of nourishment: strength and comfort, gentleness and kindness, wisdom and knowledge. And each one has his fill. **This is the Brotherhood, the new mankind, the new way of living our human nature.** No longer is it a question of being trapped by fate, inextricably, in the difficult economic contingency, but of being part of the solar contingency, where things were planned to allow life to flow down from Heaven: economy, love, policy flow miraculously, like breathing. This is the new mankind, in which sharing is the principle, each one offering his virtues, his bread, his heart, his thinking. We are the real economists, dealing with forces and qualities, energies and powers given to us by life to be used intelligently, to be cultivated and redistributed, without waste. We are the real economists, the only economists of happiness, for the famous economists who talk on television about things that have nothing to do with the heart, can't ever produce happiness. We are real economists, we are brothers. I have seen the brothers in the morning Sun, meditating, breathing, exercising their imaginations, accepting, uniting themselves with Heaven's purposes, praying, singing, sweating, working the land all day and planting the wheat and the vine. I've seen them under the worst conditions, building roads and houses that must be enlarged and improved as soon as built, to provide shelter and comfort for more and more brothers of a Brotherhood in constant expansion, artisans and companions living amid toil, effort, and strain, together in the movement of their hearts toward inner perfection.

It is in this movement that everything I have witnessed, everything about the School becomes true. Without the movement, nothing is undeniably true, nor even likely... not the bread and wine, the rose laurels, or anything else; without the movement of the heart to start with and continue on with, not even the example of the Master would seem true. The movement of the heart makes the truth absolutely true, as the Master says. The Brotherhood is absolutely true. It is the movement of survival, and it is full of joy! This is no wild exaggeration or over-idealization, it is the truth, perhaps the only truth one needs to know.


## EVOLUTION TOWARD PERFECTION:
### The Way to Joy

Joy is a sudden flowering of the heart, a dilatation, a feeling of expansion. The word itself is gay and relaxed, it writes joyfully: one is full of joy, one bursts with joy, one yells for joy! It's a shining word. Joy rises: we leap for joy! We give ourselves joyfully, we hear the joyous sound of bugles and joyful news, we are someone's joy, we are overjoyed at the sight of the one we love, we enjoy our holidays! In short, joy is good. Synonyms: cheerfulness, gladness, liveliness, delight, rejoicing, jollity, gaiety, jubilation and exteriorization. It's a merry word! To such an extent that the Master tells us: «You are better prepared to bear suffering than you are to bear the joy that lies ahead: the high vibrations of an intense joy such as you have never experienced.»


It is the total absence of joy that is so surprising to-day. A sign of the times, it is lacking. Certainly there is no joy on the faces of our scientists and philosophers and political leaders as we see them on television. Joy seems to recede as they advance! Look at the Presidents! It's this custom of joyless assemblies that worries one, joyless as the towering buildings, the grey pavements. Two people kneel to pray, sadness comes over them ; a group about to meditate settles down with sadness, as if it were more correct to be sad than joyful! As if God enjoyed sadness in His Paradise, in which case it would be more like Hell. The Initiates assure us the opposite is true. «God's holy joy», they say. And «The joy of the Lord is your strength.» And, «In Thy presence is fulness of joy...» What about His living waters that are meant to flow out of our bellies? Weigh these words of promise, and weigh yourself also. The world is dying of joylessness to-day, as one dies of drought in the desert, as other constellations and humanities and luminaries, other brotherhoods, have died... from joylessness, the joylessness of their ideal.


I lived at the Initiatic School and I experienced joy. For me it was real, joy was a reality, I felt something one feels nowhere else. Not the joy of some fleeting pleasure or other, but a state of euphoria in the heart as well as in the body, a heartfelt indescribable joy, a sudden awareness of light vibrations or as we said earlier, a **space** filled with happiness. I cannot label such happiness as «mystical» group sentimentality, but rather, as I see other beings around me all living this secret and happy state, I think it must be the movement of evolution toward perfection animating the basic cells, the foundation, of this School. Doubtless the movement has the ability to remove the burdens that keep us from being joyful, since as we know, it is only when we have no burdens that we feel light enough to plunge into a movement with joy! Look at children, they have no burdens, all they know is the evolutive movement and they rejoice all day long. The first stage of life is motion, the second stage is love (warmth), the emotional, sentimental stage that wakens with puberty, and the third stage is thought. When man is obliged to think, to figure out all his cares and difficulties, responsibilities, commitments... then life becomes complicated and joy leaves.

I remember Maître Omraam Mikhaël Aïvanhov revealing something to us one day in the Sun, something that has not been clear for two thousand years, the words of Jesus: «... except ye become as little children, ye shall not enter into the Kingdom of Heaven.» His explanation explained joy! «These words have never been properly interpreted», he said. «Everybody thinks they mean that we are to demonstrate nothing but good qualities such as candour, innocence, purity, kindness. Yes, it's true, children have many good qualities that adults have not. Children exclaim with joy over the smallest things, a pebble, an insect, a flower; when they fall, they pick themselves up; when they cry, they break quickly into laughter, and so forth. But that was not what Jesus meant. He meant that when you are a child, you are nourished, taken care of, dressed, protected, and loved; a child's burdens fall on his parents' shoulders. When the child grows up, he takes charge of his affairs himself, and that is the beginning of his worries, discouragement, sadness. Why? Because the child has become an adult. Then how is it possible, how can one remain a child in order to enter the Kingdom of God? It isn't possible, it makes no sense. However, let's think about it: if the child becomes anxious, gloomy, and disagreeable as he grows up, it is because he no longer has his parents to help and protect him. But where are his parents? Above! If we, as adults, continued to listen to our parents, to obey our Heavenly Father and do His will, then all would be well! Our Parents are above, way beyond us, we are dependent on them, and whether we know it or not it was they who sent us here, it is their help we need if we are to be protected, helped, enlightened, and happy... joyful! Do you see now why people are joyless? Because they have cut the ties with their Heavenly Parents. They no longer believe in their existence, they no longer have the loving trust and obedience of a child who puts his little hand in his mother's hand and follows her trustingly, knowing she will not lead him into danger. Isn't it time human beings understood that as long as they hold on to their pride and independence, their self-sufficiency, they will have to suffer? They must become like little children! Everyone thinks a Master is like a child: true, he is a child because he has understood that it is the way to be if you want to live in the Kingdom of God on earth, which is peace and joy. He remains obedient to his Heavenly Parents and never loses confidence in them. Ah! If only we understood that, if only we understood why a Master behaves in certain ways! People pride themselves on being in tune with the times, they think a Master's attitude is old-fashioned and ridiculous.

They are far from understanding the essential, they have stopped at appearances. A Master acts only in accordance with the higher laws and rules, the best and most efficacious for the entire world.»

I leave you to consider these words, dear reader, with no comment. How is it possible for such an immensely powerful Being to be at the same time so gentle, so humble, so soothing? It's like being surrounded by the fragrance of roses.

In grammar school, your little innocent learns other things: how to become familiar with a joyless universe, how to get used to rigidity, security. He is already set as far as his future is concerned, according to his diplomas, his badges, his desk in the front row, his classification. As he grows up he will be interested in more and more security (especially for himself), economic, sensory and political security, insurance benefits and social security, retirement funds; he will be old and sad at twenty, rigid and set in his ways, his heart hard as a pebble on the path and full of darkness, his poor heart that dreamed of other things entirely, of changing spaces and vast stretches for his imagination, and simple joys... the solar movement full of joy, which he needs, in order to survive.

And so, I have seen a Being full of joy, I have watched him live. An Initiate. He is the example, a living example. His joy comes from the evolutive movement toward spiritual and divine perfection. That is how I understand it. The perfection is in him, in us, needing only to be encouraged, increased and intensified. That is the «living water» that fills our cellular and solar spaces with joy. That is the life in the interstellar, intermolecular, and interatomic spaces. That is the active meditation of our organisms, the accelerator. It is the morning «thank you», the antidote to our tension, depression, and sadness. Try it! The Master says that once, while doing some experimentation in Alchemy in his laboratory, he discovered a product that can neutralize and disintegrate the poison of human hatreds, a product that no analytical chemist has ever discovered (a Master's «laboratory» has more elements in it than any chemist's, and is small and light and made of such fine matter, so diaphanous and invisible, that he can carry it around with him without anyone suspecting). The product he discovered that is so effective is gratitude : be grateful and give thanks all day long even if there is no reason to do so, give thanks even if you have been treated cruelly and unfairly. Is this a current habit of the religious, even among the fanatic?

That is the ingenuous message of the Initiate, today, in 1980. From having watched him live, I know what I believe in and I know what I do not believe in.


I do not believe in ready-made brotherhoods full of gloom, already doomed. I do not believe in a brotherhood which you enter easily, where membership is handed down from father to son, with the table set for dinner when you arrive ; I do not believe in planned and scheduled meetings and activities, nor in the idea of a Paradise that is there on your doorstep when you open the door, your place reserved... what a bore! Life is a solar joy in movement, as the Initiate shows us. I do not believe in the word brotherhood, or fraternity, it is dry as a desert. What I believe in is the movement of life that is a solar joy. I believe in Brotherhood as a movement of joy in action. I believe that Brotherhood is already here, in the movement of the heart, in the movement of evolution that mankind has forgotten, and that Maître Omraam Mikhaël Aïvanhov is reviving, by being himself the model of integrity and lucidity, true to the spirit of Cosmic morality.

I believe, because I saw it. I believe, because I watched him organize his Initiatic School of Brotherhood, patterned on the solar system in the heavens, so that the living currents, joyous and fraternal, could flow naturally. I believe, because I lived in this organization, and felt the movement of the three solar worlds, movements that were enlightening, warming, reviving, good for the heart, making it beat faster, illuminating one's face. I believe, because, like so many others, I see how marvellous it is, and I receive the benefits. I believe, because I have only to think of it to be flooded with joy. Yes, this idea of a collective evolution toward perfection appears to be the only way to bring us together and turn us into brothers, all of us, scientists bent on getting to the bottom of things, philosophers who have never found the solution to the problem of love, and political leaders who do not dare to be themselves, caught in circumstances where they wear a disguise, where they make promises that will not be kept, where they must pretend, lie, scheme, and manœuver to attain what they want : their own prestige, their «honour».

I submit to your heart the following thought of an Initiate, Maître Omraam Mikhaël Aïvanhov, for its consideration.

«Until mankind is able to accept the Initiatic Teaching, which reveals the existence of a higher realm more real than the lower one, we will never have a great political leader, nor will we ever have a really great economist, because there will

always be the motive of personal interest behind their projects, the desire to dominate, to calculate in favour of themselves, to seek revenge, etc... and under those conditions,
there can never be any happiness for the people. Of course,
they know how to disguise their real motives, they know the
forms and gestures to make, they know the right things to say
about what is best for the country and what will make the
happiness of mankind, etc... but if they were to appear in
their true light with all their greed and inferior tendencies,
you and I know that no one would approve, and they know it
also... that is why they bluff and lie and lead us... where? Fortunately, everyone is not that way. Many are devoted, sincere,
honest, noble and of great value to humanity, but they are
generally prevented from carrying out their plans. With the
light of the Teaching of the Great Universal White Brotherhood and with more people like that, it would be possible to
realize the Golden Age on earth, happiness for the whole
world at last, and at last, peace.

If you are looking for someone with completely unselfish
motives, someone who is really noble and sublime, you will
have to find an Initiate : you have to hope and pray that the
Initiates will come and help us. They who have purified
themselves, who have proved themselves, who have suffered,
who have conquered and won : they are the ones to transform
the world.»


The idea of evolution being the only thing that gives life
meaning, the only «contingency», seems to us who know the
Maître the only solution, the only way to have the «just and
lasting peace» mankind is looking for. We have lived this idea
of collective respiration, the movement of the heart that unifies, the yeast that draws everything together, the emanation,
vibration and radiation that spread sunlight everywhere and
bring life to the community ; we think of it as a flowering

(celestial vanity if you will), but most of all, we think of it as the brotherly joy that takes people who are complicated and simplifies them. And unifies them. I agree that the power of this School comes from the Master's joy, or is the joy in his aura... who knows? But I also feel it is this brotherly and joyous spirit, this «movement» that awakens men's souls and allow people as dissimilar as you can find to live and sing together. For me, that is the most important aspect of the genius of Maître Omraam Mikhaël Aïvanhov, knowing how to launch the movement of the heart, when everywhere else the movement of the head, the mind and intellect, is emphasized to the point of turning people to dust. His genius is to make people live and work and sing together, to make them unite in the same current and the same joy, people who are entirely different... those who work with their minds, those who work with their hearts, and those who work with their hands, all equally essential (including the pride and self-sufficiency of the intellectual, the egocentricity of the sentimental, the authoritativeness of the strong-willed). The head, the heart, the body are equally necessary; those who think, those who love, and those who organize, are equally necessary; those who make a noise and those who keep the silence, those who stimulate and those who enervate,... all vitally necessary for life to be able to circulate and flow along with the problems, all necessary for the survival of the whole, the collective whole.* The genius of Maître Omraam Mikhaël Aïvanhov is in enabling the people who trust him to live, sing and work together in the same joy, realising brotherhood... by giving it to them! **He creates a new type of man.** Perfected man, free of hypocrisy, ready to sacrifice his will to violence for the will to love,

* It must be understood that a collective body (society) functions in the same way our body functions, with certain cells for the head, certain other cells for the heart, and still more for the body, forming all together the metabolism that keeps the body alive. Some cells even serve as drains or sewers, to get rid of the waste, by gossip and pettiness, for instance.

because of the movement; call it what you will, vanity of vanities, anything... the important thing is that you allow the movement to enter you and improve you.


## EVOLUTION TOWARD PERFECTION:
### The Authority or a World Government

The World Government, the **Initiatic** plan for World Government is announced for sometime before the end of the present century.* We might pray to make things move ahead more quickly, we might think of nothing else and talk of nothing else and announce the good news with ringing of bells: the time is near. But should we reveal what Maître Omraam Mikhaël Aïvanhov has told us about this tremendous project? I asked him that question, and he assented.


Here, therefore, are the revelations. No doubt they will be overwhelming to men of good will. I hope so. Maybe others, those who suffer but who don't want to change, will also be convinced. People have reached a point where they are so unbelieving, so opposed, so suspicious and critical, they have to analyse and tear everything apart in order to be certain; one has to give proof after proof in order to convince the people who are most in need of help! But this is to be expected: during the era of the Fish, Pisces, which we are just coming out of, faith ruled, one simply believed, without further explanation... until doubt came. In the era of Aquarius, which we are just coming into, the Master is all the explanation we need; the revelations you are about to read will prove that, and at the same time show you that I am not unduly preju-

* See «Before the End of the Century...» by the author.

Views of the Camp

diced or spellbound. Or, if spellbinding means as it says in the dictionary, to «exert an irresistible attraction», it's true, I do feel irresistibly attracted to the explanations the Master gives us. I have listened to all kinds of people and I am fairly particular as far as authenticity and truth are concerned. In politics, for instance, obviously what you hear is not true, it doesn't ring true, one has a right to be suspicious, we don't know which «saint» to vote for! But when you find a Being who opens your eyes and proves to you he has found the answers simply by reading the living book of Nature, by observing Heaven and earth, and proves it by showing you a host of things you have never noticed, what do you do? Aren't you obliged to follow him? Wouldn't you follow him? He interprets the little things of everyday life so simply and clearly, so differently from the way we do; I mean, he makes things mathematically clear, all the links and correspondences become obvious and logical.

For instance, he doesn't stop at the three words, light, love and life, which correspond with our infinite needs, as we have said; he goes further and shows where the correspondences lead to: light corresponds to thinking, in the brain; love (warmth) corresponds to breathing and circulation in the heart and lungs; life corresponds to nourishment and digestion in the stomach.* Making it is easy to understand the daily methods practised at the School, which I have described earlier.

A human being is a trinity in the likeness of God, he thinks, he feels, he acts. The correspondences go all the way to infinity. For instance, under the heading of light come science, philosophy, knowledge, learning; under the heading of love come religion, ethics, morality; under the heading of life come movement, creation, realization, art.

---

* Stomach, in Russian, is «jivot» and in Bulgarian, «jivot» means life.

Maître Omraam Mikhaël Aïvanhov's message to mankind is that everything can be marvellous and that the Golden Age can come on earth once we understand where our interest lies, and that our function corresponds with the Sun's function: to give light, to give heat, to bring life. Since a collective body functions no differently from our own bodies, where (I repeat) light is to be found in the brain, warmth and communication in the lungs and heart, and life and exchanges in the stomach... this Master, with his science of correspondences, goes so far as to disclose a plan for a perfect government, based on light (wisdom), warmth (love and kindness), and life (movement and truth).

If we want the world to live in peace and plenty, the requirements are as follows:

1. People who are enlightened to represent the Authority, who are advanced in the realm of light, and who have given proof of their knowledge (wisdom).

2. People who are capable of judging correctly, impersonally, equitably, to represent Justice and the Law, beyond prejudice and influence (love).

3. People of integrity to represent the Economy to control and distribute finances as the energy in the body is controlled and distributed by the digestive process (life).

Or:

1. One Authority, to dominate, guide, and advise on all issues: the level of education, universities, institutes, religion.

2. One Power, subject to the Authority: the level of law, judges and magistrates.

3.   One Economy : the material level.


This Government could bring peace, plenty, joy and harmony to the world, a Golden Age such as the world knew once before, during the reign of Ram, 7,400 years before Christ. It lasted 3,500 years!


Following the Sun's example there would be three Hierarchies :

**1.   The Authority**

Education, religion, the press, all media, etc.

**2.   The Power**

Magistrature, legislation, administration, Police, Armed Forces, etc...

**3.   The Economy**

Currency, banking, stock and trade exchange, real estate, agriculture, manufacturing, employment, commerce, syndicates, etc...


This system of government is called *synarchy*. Sooner or later, humans (those who are left) will have no other recourse but to establish it. In the meanwhile, the thing that keeps them from accepting it is their ignorance. They don't know why Cosmic Intelligence conceived things as they are; they don't know how completely the Sun conforms to Cosmic Intelligence, nor why; and they cannot see that the Sun shows us very clearly how to conform, ourselves... because human beings are so concentrated on their personal and narrow little affairs. They are interested only in their own ambition, their own success, their own control and domination, their own privilege and front row seats. The last thing that interests them is the way Cosmic Intelligence has organized the Universe.

Where do politics belong in the Hierarchy? How can politics keep our lives on the right road unless they are based on the Cosmic order as demonstrated by the Sun? Is it possible to govern people without light? I mean, without the Initiatic Science, without knowing human nature and the laws that govern the Universe? No, not on your life. Therefore, politics belong in the first Hierarchy along with education and the Teaching. Is it possible to judge others correctly if one is not honest and full of love and integrity oneself? No! Is it possible to be a «wise and faithful steward ruling over the household» correctly, if one has no idea of the needs and requirements, the failings and weaknesses of human beings?

I took down these notes while sitting beside Maître Omraam Mikhaël Aïvanhov. I hand them on to you with all due respect for something sacred: a sacred vision of the future. He speaks in the mathematically precise language of a Master; such precision is proof enough that he is incapable of deceiving people, taking advantage of them or casting spells on them! He is not talking about himself, he is not inventing this system or anything else; he is not affected by our way of doing things, our human, changeable laws; he is interested only in stating the Cosmic Truth. His aim is on the highest possible level of disinterestedness: help people to survive. And since you would also like things to be different from the way they are, I invite you to participate in the same work, to collaborate with him. Begin simply by taking a pencil and a clean piece of paper: make three columns, one for light, one for love, one for life, and inscribe in each column what you have just read. You will then have in hand the new society and the way in which the World Government will operate. Only the names are lacking! Isn't it wonderful? And since it is the Golden Age, with true «Liberty, Equality, Fraternity» for all concerned, you must admit it is worth taking a minute of your time to study this plan. It is your future.


Three things become apparent.

1.   In the right order: Light, Love, Life. Alas, our human systems begin with the economy, running counter-current to Heaven, and leaving no doubt as to the way the world is going... toward a catastrophe. We are all hypnotized by economics, our leaders most of all. Such things as statistics, percentages, market forecasts, business relations, international official visits for the purpose of selling... are all well and good, but not if the order of importance is reversed, not if the reversal produces the desperate bottleneck the world is in now. The world with its worries and domestic strife, difficulties, unemployment and violence, plus the great fear that all our acquired social advantages might soon disappear, has nothing more to look forward to but the day the bills fall due. The Initiates propose to put things in their right order – «on earth as it is in Heaven» – Light, Love, Life. The Economy (Life) depends on moral ethics (Love), which in turn depend on Philosophy (Light).* The economic power depends on the legislative power which depends on the executive power. Yes, at the head of everything, the Executive Power of the Sages, which carries out the Cosmic Programme: Evolution toward Perfection. Humans put the Economy above everything, and stop there. If they think they can ever stabilize the Economy,

* See «Before the End of the Century» by the same author.

which is composed of things that belong to everyday life, to movement, to the periphery, to our metabolism and all the natural existing oppositions, if they hope to stabilize the basic undercurrents and undertow, with **Economics...** what ignorance! What madness! Madness to think you can extract happiness and joie de vivre (which belong to the realm of the heart) from economics!

2.   Back to the heart once more: note that the law-makers and magistrates are men of heart, chosen especially for their capacity for goodness and kindness, their love of humanity. What a wonderful solution to all the problems of justice and administration! We who wonder where to classify love, well, that is where it belongs, in legislature, in offices. Laws based on kindness as well as justice! A Golden Age indeed.

3.   The system is universal, as you have seen. Now, when men are given power, the first thing they do is to gather their supporters around them and form a political clique as a bulwark against the opposition, they attract as many followers as possible with all kinds of promises... we are all familiar with the system. The Initiates on the other hand, want to unite all men, of all races, all languages, all beliefs, all uniforms, all parties, politics and religious persuasions. Everyone will work together under one universal authority for: the evolution toward perfection!

Of course you don't believe all this, you are too used to doubting. «How will the Initiates ever be able to do that?» you think. «How can they change men's minds so radically, so quickly?» That isn't the point. The point is that there are certain currents of force now in movement. To-day's economic hypnosis is leading to an impasse because it isn't able to satisfy the heart or meet its needs, and the result of dissatisfaction is violence... it has already begun. The time is coming when no one will listen to anyone anymore, when no world leader will be credible. What then? Well, before long, because of the need for survival, because of the force of circumstances, men of goodwill will find themselves having to summon the Initiates.

If it is true that we will be calling on the Initiates before long, we should begin immediately to try and understand that they use forces to modify form as Nature does, from one season to the next. That is where they learn their extraordinary patience. I have seen this done by a Master who is a true revolutionary, that is, a Being who doesn't hesitate to shatter the old forms violently and impatiently, because he relies entirely on the new currents and the solar authority. He is conscious of time and space, of cause and effect, and he works with principles. That is why he will be able to install the Golden Age among men. You see that the Initiates, in their plan for World Government, use all the existing forms of power and economics to a really surprising extent. Then what is new about their plan? The solar authority. The Initiates count on that to do away gradually with the old forms and replace them with other forms unknown to us now... as, in the days of the stage-coach, no one knew how to communicate by satellite. Politicians in the news to-day act entirely contrarily to that: whether they call themselves leftists or rightists, they are still in the old forms, criticizing and insulting each other, each trying to annihilate the other form of government, left and right! But they all bow to the same authority: materialism! Meaning that the old forms are preserved and revolts and massacres repeat themselves... the victims and the executioners merely change places. That has been the history of mankind for a thousand years. Initiates start out by condemning the old forms, but the thing they count on to do away with the old forms is the new form... solar authority, and the currents from Heaven.

Maître Omraam Mikhaël Aïvanhov says: «The Great Universal White Brotherhood is constantly sending out currents of unity into the world. For those who are already prepared, it will be easy to seize these currents and do something with them, at last. That will be the most wonderful day in human history, the whole earth will become one family, the billions in world currency that go down the drain for arms and weapons, espionage, etc. will be used to transform the earth into Paradise. Right now we find these ideas Utopian, but one day they will be realized. To everyone's surprise, they will catch on and be accepted by the entire world. If not, human beings will disappear from the face of the earth, the events will see to that. The forming of a Pan-Europe, a Pan-Asia, a Pan-America or a Pan-Africa is progress, to be sure, but only a Pan-World can solve all the problems. If they are not solved, it will no longer be one country against the other, it will be continent against continent, Asia against Europe. Will that be better?»

## EVOLUTION TOWARD PERFECTION:
### Spiritual Alchemy*

«Whatever we do, we should always think about doing it from the Sun's point of view. For instance, you might say: I

---

* Author's note: We are now fairly well along on the path of evolution. I am not concerned here with whether man is a fallen angel or a privileged monkey, that is an aspect of evolution that belongs to scientists. Perhaps one day they will say that man is not angelic, that monkey is the fallen man, which seems more likely. What is certain is that man has the role, on the path of evolution toward perfection, the task of changing the mammalian programme dictated by his brain, for reasons of survival, from the programme of materialism (egocentric and biocentric, based on pleasure and acquisition) to a Cosmic, collective, heliocentric programme (based on joy and the will to give) which is what our spiritual brain needs. It is the only

love this girl, I really love her. But if I express my love, what does it mean for her? Will it mean enlightenment or darkness? Will it be perturbing to her? Will my love bring her joy, inspiration, happiness? Or will it bring grief and woe and disillusion? Will my love be stimulating for her, a reviving force that will keep her well and healthy, or will it exhaust her, harm her in some way?

If we prefaced everything with the question: Am I bringing light, am I bringing encouragement and energy, am I a good influence, then everyone's life would be changed. Instantly. Are there many who think this way?»

These were the words of light, love and life that I heard one spring morning. Maître Omraam Mikhaël Aïvanhov included everything in that question; I don't know any better feeling than when one finds the answer in one's heart. All young girls are fresh and clear they become beautiful princesse, and all young men are gods. It magnifies everything. If we were always asking ourselves, am I enlightening others, am I being warm and encouraging, am I bringing life to this person, it would change our lives.

The science of the movement of the heart is called spiritual Alchemy. With this science, now unknown to man, Maître Omraam Mikhaël Aïvanhov opens up the realm of real PSI power.

---

programme that will allow him to resolve his group problems. To do it, he needs a science. The science of Spiritual Alchemy is therefore given to him at this particular moment in history, because without this pursuit of evolution and perfection, man is condemned to disppear by bio-holocaust, the result of his inability to stand the new Cosmic currents of Aquarius now beginning to appear. Man is not the first of the great mammals to have disappeared.

Alchemy? Visions of the Middle Ages, fires burning on the hearth, melting pots and ironworks and red flames against the night sky; names such as Nicholas Flamel, Trevisan, Sendivogius, Riple, John Dee, Basile Valentin, Paracelsus; a science devoted to the study of life and the transformation of raw metals into gold, the science of the subtle: Alchemists sought the Philosophic Stone, the Elixir of Eternal Life, the Universal Panacea, all magic substances. And take the word magic: in its true sense it denotes the noble power of healing, the power to postpone death indefinitely, the power to open up a higher state of consciousness... in short, it means something out of the ordinary... the science of the marvellous. And here is a live Master (alive in our day!) talking about Spiritual Alchemy!

Spiritual? Yes, but not Nicholas Flamel's burning fires and melting pots, no red flames in the night; now the fire is in us, the flames are our love, the fire is our fervour, delivering the nights from fear. Lead is still being transformed into gold, but the gold is in our hearts; it is still a question of going from darkness into light, but the light is in your hearts. We still rise from the roots to the corolla, but we utilize the sap and juices of the heart to create a movement of evolution that stirs the whole heart... the lower side as well as the higher side, the lunar side along with the solar side. It is a question of setting fire to our hearts, a glowing fire that will transmute all that is base and lowly into something ablaze with light, something marvellous... a science indeed unknown to man, originating somewhere else...

This is the way I see this Being (surely come from some other planet?). He uses Alchemy on the forces of his heart to testify to the light, to create a solar atmosphere on earth. This is all he thinks about. He comes to us no doubt from Agarttha, that marvellous country of antiquity (still alive in the traditions of certain Nordic countries, and in Initiatic story-books)* where all creatures lived by the science of eternal light, eternal youth, eternal love. His face reflects eternal youth and eternal love; his attitude shows that he has discovered the secret of how to transform his will to violence into the will to love; he dominates the impulsive current, controlling fear and the shadows with a firm hand... in other words, he has solar power. What a dynamic lesson to be able to watch this spectacle! I wonder about one thing. If he didn't use spiritual Alchemy on his own physical matter, what would he do about the violent, primordial force which in his case would be impossible to evaluate... the sexual force? How far we've come from our catechism lessons! I don't believe any more in the pale gentleness of Jesus... he must have had more than that in order to bear his Cross... and if this Master left one day for some other planet, there to act out his solar role before other creatures less indifferent than humans, the last idea I would have of him that would stay with me forever, to be my hope each dawn, would be the image of the Archangel overcoming the Dragon. Meaning that everything I have seen this Master do and say is indescribable, really; the immeasurable greatness of the consciousness of an Initiate is too far beyond the feeble consciousness of man. His vision of space and time, the authenticity of his example, the grandeur and nobleness of his heart, are enough to contain several solar systems.

Two examples of the Master's use of Alchemy: in the daily life of his School, the routine, as they say, the Master has a magistral way of handling people, he involves them in tasks that are grandiose and way beyond them... whereupon, if they rise to the occasion, they develop a taste for the grandiose and

---

* «The Knights of the Round Table», «The Childhood of Lancelot», etc.

the marvellous, and... they evolve! This way of educating people to surpass themselves is nothing short of inspired. A transcendental form of pedagogy. The essence of Alchemy. He knows how to put authority in the hands of those whose wills to violence would otherwise jeopardize his creation, the gigantic task he has undertaken. He puts them in a top position and leaves them free to express themselves, apparently against all reason. And you see these people, shown up **to themselves** by the force of circumstance and their new responsibilites, actually becoming liberated, gradually letting themselves be affected by the powerful Alchemy of the School's currents, until they are transformed. Evolving! Their faces take on the golden hue of the Sun. Or if not, if they are unable to transmute their will to violence, they disappear of their own accord, quite naturally. Whatever happens, they are aware of the power of the Initiate, the seed is planted.

This is the prototype of the revolutionary education of the new era. No great man in history ever used his power this way. People like Fouquet, imprisoned for life at Pignerol, or the Duke d'Enghien, shot at Vincennes for instance, paid for their uprisings with their lives, and history was tarnished for nothing; as seen from above in the invisible world, in the permanence of life, nothing was solved, the people in conflict remained in conflict, enemies to the end.


In 1947, Maître Omraam Mikhaël Aïvanhov received the visit of a person of considerable importance whom I will not name, so as not to be connected in any way with him or his name that was repeated often enough by the newspapers. The master told us to receive this person with kindness, knowing in advance by intuition that he would bring us nothing but trouble. When he arrived in all his importance, my friends and I greeted him effusively, naively. The Master played his role of great Initiate and solar magus. He gave Judas every chance. The play unfolded. The dramatic events that followed will be part of history one day. However disastrous the events, however much suffering they imposed on the Master, in the end they were one more proof of his knowledge, and the magic of his Alchemy, which he used to transform the darkness of those events into light, and his terror into love. Everything that he predicted was realized. And what happened to him? He transformed himself! What happened to the powerful personality who claimed to be under the protection of high personages all over the world?... he died sometime later in Spain under the most dire circumstances. And no one could save him.

How can we not understand then, that spiritual Alchemy is the means whereby we can make something miraculous of our lives? We can believe in miracles, not only miracles in the remote Catholic tradition, but miracles today, now, in the street and in the marketplace, the miracle of becoming solar mages ourselves! Face to face with a Being such as the Master, we can never say: «My life is thus and so and will never be anything else.» The Master shows us that our hearts are capable of changing anything and everything once we know how to turn shadows into light, once we acquire magic ability from the Sun at sunrise, once we learn how to drink the Sun in the perpetuity of our successive lives. Without the sublimation of love, how would it be possible for the Golden Age to come on earth, to bring us, while politicians rattle on, to the «just and lasting peace» men dream about?

The Master gives us also the practical side of the new science of Spiritual Alchemy.* Each day we create our «inner life», we develop awareness, a sudden coming of age, as the

* See «Spiritual Alchemy» Volume II, Complete Works, Omraam Mikhaël Aïvanhov.

«children» we create are sent out into space (our thoughts and feelings are our creations, are they not?). We are even proud of this paternity. Even if these children are only electromagnetic waves (at the very least), they are bound to have an effect, either for good or for evil, according not only to their quality and character, but the quality and character of the heart that gave them birth. Thus we reach a high peak in the flowering that is the Master's plan for us. The creative work we perform inwardly at every instant of every day fills us with new responsibility... Cosmic responsibility! We know that our thoughts and feelings, our children, even our secret, irregular children, are living entities, and, depending on their character, they are bearers of love or violence. This is something that never occurred to us before. Now, we think about it, we take care to practise spiritual Alchemy, turning them into Suns before releasing them on the world. Since there are several billion men to be affected in this way, the result could be incalculable, making the world into a Paradise or into Hell. There is good reason for many of the existing conditions and for the black tide rising in our consciousness.

But those are not the only children. Maître Omraam Mikhaël Aïvanhov is realistic, he knows that universal brotherhood is not something that will happen in a day. He knows that if he teaches spiritual Alchemy to prospective mothers, the children conceived by them will be born fully prepared. A child is the product of a marvellous Alchemist: his mother. The Master reveals what modern scientists are only beginning to suspect, that a mother has the power, bestowed on her by Nature, to produce either a genius or a criminal: she transmutes lead into gold in her laboratory, the womb! This is the crucial point of the solar revolution that the Initiates are preparing.

This is nothing our political leaders discovered. It is the answer to the question: how do the Initiates plan to change the mentality of mankind? By what miracle? It is simple, like all miracles. One day, mankind will come to the conclusion that it has been led astray by prejudice and partiality, economic ignorance and shortsightedness. It will be at an impasse, unable to advance because of its unresolved problems, unable to provide the materials on which the present life-system is based, unable to stop the dissatisfaction, misery, and violence on the part of the people, or the ecological manifestations on the parts of Nature, not to mention other unknown contributing Cosmic events. At that point, a few individuals will know enough to summon the Initiates, their superiors in the Hierarchy, and ask for help. The Initiates will come, they will bring their programme for world government by Synarchy as described above, and they will put it in action. The social organization of the world will change, another ambiance will invade the atmosphere, attracting beneficent Cosmic currents, presences and entities. Fear and violence will be forced back into their caves. We will breathe again. But our human mentality cannot change in a twinkling, a day, or even a century... it takes a number of successive lives to transform a civilization.

Mothers are the ones who will have the task of transforming mankind, by their thoughts and their attitude during pregnancy, they will be able to transform man in three generations... an unbelievably important, magic, **Cosmic** task. How many times have I heard a young mother say that she recognized in the way her child behaved and thought, the exact same thinking, the same attitude she had while carrying the child? During pregnancy a mother's thoughts, if she uses Alchemy on her inner life, can have a great bearing on the child's beauty, health, solar affinity. A prodigious role, a prophetic mission, the role of womanhood. But as it is now, does a mother ever think that the child she is carrying will grow up to be in part responsible for the world's welfare and that she must try to produce a genius? The time has come when we need benefactors and Initiates and geniuses instead of madmen if we are to do anything for mankind.


Today when I am asked, «Who is this Master?» I answer: he is the example of the new man. He eats fire and he drinks the light! Why not seize the historic opportunity to learn from him? The world is cracking, split apart by our critical, analytical, greedy behaviour within the family or the party, where war always starts, in the family, in the party, and... worse... in ourselves, the real seat of the trouble. We live with a sharp and painful fissure within ourselves between light and darkness, we are in contradiction with our own flesh, and when we finally dare to try to see each other in the light of the Sun, something within opposes us, even then. That is where war begins. How can we not, therefore, seize the opportunity now available to us to learn this science that unifies the heart and brings peace and harmony. The disciples of Maître Omraam Mikhaël Aïvanhov live by this new science, I have seen them. To achieve brotherhood, they rely more on the «movement of the heart» than on any rules or methods for living together. That is the secret of spiritual Alchemy, the wish above all else to have the «movement of the heart», to eat fire and to drink light! And for this Master of the Initiatic School, the movement of the heart counts more than any method, for the movement permits us to live together in unity, whereas methods divide people. As in the Church to-day, for instance. Division leads to death. The universal method that Maître Omraam Mikhaël Aïvanhov proposes serves to create unity and the «movement of the heart». Eat fire, and drink light! His disciples count more on the path of Brotherhood itself than on the way they place their feet. They use

Entrance to the Fire Area

The Ceremony of the Fire at the Festival of Michaelmas

work, any work, to throw themselves into the «movement of the heart». Appreciation and admiration are born of the «movement of the heart», thus proving that true spirituality is not the discarding of matter and everything physical, nor is it restricted to prayer and meditation... no. Rather it is the spiritualization of matter, for everything can be spiritual, the heart, the body, the brain, the work we do. Every spiritual function is beautiful and everything is pale or sordid without spirituality, including genius. The high purpose of the solar revolution of men's minds is the eating of fire and the drinking of light.

Yes, if spiritual Alchemy, the new science, is indeed this secret movement, this blazing fire that transforms our will to violence into the will to love, if harmony between brothers begins there, then I have seen men and women put this theory into practice successfully, drawing on its light for the beauty of their lives. I have seen this science work successfully in the way they look at each other, in what they say to each other, in their gestures; three effective ways: the way they look at each other links them to the world of light, at sunrise; by the way they speak, they communicate with each other in the world of love; by their gestures, they experience the world of brotherhood, making bread and wine together, working together in fertilizer and cement, building roads, vibrating all the time together. I have seen it. They are the solar artisans of Aquarius, the ones who know how to do everything with the heart from baking bread to prayer, forming a Brotherhood with their own hands without waiting for others to become brotherly. No more will they accept blindly to pattern themselves on television stars (nor to adopt their philosophy), nor to be guided against all reason by the speeches of distinguished intellectuals or the ineffectual dreams of sentimentalists or the stupid resignation of robots. They will understand that man must use Alchemy on his vital forces in order to keep renewing the movement of his heart. They are the artisans of the future, living the example of a living Master, people whose first concern is the movement of perfection in their hearts. Fire and light! Motivation! **The new romanticism of Aquarius!** The point of reference, the philosophy, the dream, in practice. People will control physical matter through their intellects, feelings and actions, to such an extent that today's materialists will be flabbergasted. Elementary problems such as daily bread for all the children of the world, the economy, communications, energy, will be handled easily and subtly. Daily life will be satellized, divinized, glorified, and glorifying. Theirs will be the secret exaltation that lifts one beyond time and space, theirs the knowledge of spiritual Alchemy that transmutes the will to violence into the will to love: theirs the ability to live in Paradise and direct the forces of Hell from there, transforming the dense matter and brute force of their subterranean roots. Call this «movement of the heart» love or anything you like, but pray that it may come to you and bring you joy!

Life, the movement of love; love, the movement of life... Life, Love, God, are all the same: «Only the love of God gives abundant life»! The phrase comes to mind quite naturally, it flows from the Spring. I have heard it so often, ten thousand times or more during the four seasons of summer at the Bonfin. I have tasted it in the great dyonisiac winds, sipped it in the heat of day like nectar; I've felt it in the heartbeat of this Initiatic School, a light breath of romance, a plainsong like a cool wave in the heat, carried by a thousand voices in unison. It fills the great light Hall to overflowing, shines on the Camp, lights up the rose-laurel along the paths. You hear it everywhere, a rising tide, a shining sea, a moving ocean. I like to hear it from far off, at the other end of Camp, when the Hall is full: «Only the love of God gives abundant life!» Three times over, a mantra, once for light, once for love, once for life. To think, to love, to create. «Only the love of God...» I try to imagine the God Who unites us all with one gift : Life. Life, God, Love are one and the same. Because of those three things we (and everything else) survive on earth. And if love is to ensure the survival of others, the words sing out to us that we are all alive because of the same symphonic and fraternal movement, with everything depending on Brotherhood, God, Love, and Life. You too, my brother. «Only the love of God...» I imagine God as a Light that sends great waves of warmth toward me and I hear my heart beating naturally, biologically, spiritually. «Only the love of God...» the blood courses with each heartbeat, each God-beat, penetrating my veins and arteries, my whole body to the end of my fingers, to the mobility of my hands and the goodness of my feet. «Only the love of God...» I imagine God's love for me, without which I would be nothing, less than nothing, and because He gives it to me, I can touch, taste, feel, hear, see (Oh, God) I can see the colours of life and smell its fragrance and hear its music, and taste the morning joys, and touch your hand, my brother, I can see you in your Sun, I can eat this fire and drink this light... I can speak, I can say : thank you.

# EPILOGUE

# FOR THE TIME OF THE PROPHET APPROACHES*

* «...but of that day and hour knoweth no man, no not the angels of Heaven, but my Father only. But as the days of Noah were, so shall also the coming of the Son of man be. For as in the days that were before the flood they were eating and drinking, marrying and giving in marriage, until the day that Noah entered into the ark, and knew not until the flood came and took them all away; so shall also the coming of the Son of man be...»

*St. Matthew 24:36*

## THE COSMIC HIERARCHY

The thing that keeps us from believing in the Cosmic Hierarchy is our pride. An attitude, a fatal refusal, a fatal sneer, that will cost us dear before long. We cannot tolerate the thought of anything higher, no hierarchy exists for us. «It's impossible,» we say, «an intolerable idea.» Proving how incoherent we are, for we are surrounded by hierarchies, everything in our lives is hierarchical. To survive, for instance, we need water rather than potatoes: a hierarchy; and air rather than water. We breathe eighteen times in a minute, we drink somewhat less, and eat less than we drink. Most of all we need the Sun (heat) each instant for our heart to beat 72 beats a minute without ever skipping one: a hierarchy, the hierarchy of survival, Fire, Air, Water, Earth, and above all, the Sun. You see how well planned it is, how coherent. The Sun forms the hierarchies. Water, for example, is entirely different in form and scope depending on whether it is steam at the Equator or ice at the North Pole. In the form of steam, it makes all kinds of machines work: hierarchy! Colours, sounds, flowers, caterpillars, butterflies, the species, the spaces, are all in relation to the Sun. And men also. According to their inner Sun, the power of their imagination, their

ability to enlighten and warm and stimulate others, men are
either great or small, chosen or not. If chosen, a hierarchy
forms around them immediately. They have their court, their
ministers. Their law and morals, those who are for them and
those who are against, the cops and robbers, the good and the
bad, all are connected with and depend on a certain sun for
their heartbeats. Both the genius and the masses. And why
stop there? Above and beyond the hierarchy we know, might
there not be other, unknown Beings who are more powerful
than humans, more sensitive, subtler, faster, warmer, more
luminous and more stimulating, with intense auric, ultrahigh,
ultraviolet vibrations, Beings who have gone in their hearts as
high as possible, as high as the Sun, and are able to grasp life
and history before we can, grasp the beginning? «In the beginning was the Word...» Go and see! These Beings, these
Initiates, these Chosen, went. That is the difference between
them and us, the Hierarchy. We may not recognize them, but
they recognize those above them by name, the ten Hierarchies
on the Sephirotic ladder of the Kabbala. Beings that are
higher than they! Truly the great spaces of the heart! How do
they recognize them? I really don't know. They have only
told us that the highest of all Initiates, the Teacher of Initiates, is Melchizedech.

Thinking back over the Initiates in history, one realizes
that a hierarchy exists there also... which helps us to understand the time of the Prophet now approaching. They are so
far above us, naturally we can only see these things from
down below; we must choose our words carefully and make it
clear that if we talk about lesser and greater Initiates, they are
«lesser» only in relation to «greater» and not because of any
judgment on my part. I will venture this: there are the Beings
who have been initiated in order to perform certain tasks at a
certain time; there are the Great Initiates of all time; and
there is the Prophet whose time is coming.

Among the first (the lesser?), there is still another distinction to be made between those of the intellect, those of the heart, and those of the helping hand. Some were better equipped to sense the light at the beginning... Nostradamus, for instance, and since then, Papus, Schuré, and others. They had the ability and the desire to write down what their minds knew to be true, and present it to humans for their enlightenment. Their works are important, they are a reference. Others felt the message in their souls intuitively, with warmth of feeling: they were the saints, mystics, and martyrs who gave their lives for an idea, for Jesus, for God, for the love of Love. They spoke from the heart, their faces transfigured. Saint Teresa of the Christ-Child comes to mind, and Father Foucault, two contemporaries whom I think of as having the same smile, the same renunciation and the same sacrificial death. Others armed with strong wills and the need for action became involved in the history of mankind by rising up in public and declaring the great Initiatic truths. I am thinking of two who died at the stake one hundred years apart, burned alive by Ecclesiastics, the two knights that appeal to me so much, Jeanne D'Arc and the Master of the Knights Templar. I think of Domrémy. Those are the «lesser» ones? Imagine!

The Great Initiates came to stir man's interest in his own evolution. Knowing that it is not people who are in charge of their own destinies, but the Great Initiates, working through the people. Their role is inscribed in the history of civilizations: they brought knowledge to mankind, they were the great Teachers such as Pythagoras and Socrates, the two Greeks who died for their schools, in the time before the Prophet.

Then, above them, there is the Prophet. The Prophet! A prophet, says the dictionary, is one who delivers the divine Word and prophesies future divine manifestations. A prophet intervenes when there is a decision in Heaven, such as a new season for mankind... such as the new solar revolution, the new civilization that occurs each time the vernal point enters another constellation in the Zodiac. A Prophet is the sign of a new era. For this fabulous role, I can see why it must be a Being come from elsewhere. There was Buddha for the Buddhists, Mohammed for the Mohammedans, Moses for the Jews, Jesus for the Christians. All carried in their hearts the mark of the solar spirit, the Christ. Through Christ they were put in charge of the new civilization, for (once again) it is not countries or people who bring about their evolution, or scientists, or philosophers, or academics, nor, certainly, politicians, who do no more than follow the leader. There has always been a Prophet at the beginning of every civilization, to recognize the Cosmic currents and tell others how to use them. Faced with the animality of our human consciousness, they kept themselves inaccessible to the masses, and interpreted the law of Heaven from a distance... like divinities. As man's evolution progressed, they accepted to become more and more humanized, literally placing themselves in men's hands. Certainly six thousand years ago, Hermes, the great Egyptian Initiate in the age of Taurus, protected by the Pyramids and the Hierarchy within, must have appeared as a divinity to the fellahin working along the banks of the Nile. Today his Caduceus denotes a doctor's car, no more. Hermes! who could contemplate his glory? Perhaps a few rare disciples, those who were hardy enough to survive the bitter trials of Initiation at the hands of exacting Hierophants. Around four thousand years ago, in the era of Aries, Moses, the Great Initiate, made himself accessible, compromised himself, exposed himself to danger, and fled into the desert. At the head of his people. Where he literally handed them the Tables of the Law. Two thousand years later, in the era of Pisces, Jesus became man. «Et homo factus est», sings the Roman liturgy. A man, a Fish, projected into the ocean of the world. You know what happened. Now, the new position of the earth brings us to the era of Aquarius. New solar forces will explode in space. The time has come for the new Prophet.

Whether we believe in him or not changes nothing as far as Heaven is concerned, the role of the marvellous Being who will launch the era of Aquarius is already defined. It is the era of the solar ideal, the time when the seed, having taken root in the ground, will lift itself all the way to the Sun. Evolution!

The time is now, the evolution is ours. We are about to make the transition, swept along on the currents of Aquarius, we will leave our mammalian brains behind in the prairies and fly through space to our solar brains. We need an image: the Great Initiate will be the model for mankind. This Prophet will be like Moses, like Hermes, like Jesus, like Krishna, but he will be more. He will be human, he will literally put himself within our reach and comprehension. An Initiate our model, think how marvellous, how sacred and historic that is! Initiating man in his image and resemblance! Gone the era of the angry God, the implacable Judge who had to be implored and bribed when rain was needed, or bread; gone also the era of the good father God, who left his people in misery, in shadows of ignorance where they prayed without understanding. «Thou shalt not...» But what **shall** we? We still don't know. The new era is coming: we are going to meet it with hearts more ready to accept than they seem, and the Initiate is ready to fill them! Live, a live model showing us that we have come of age and can do anything we want! With the sixth great advance of our Age (we are now entering the sixth Race in the history of humanity under the sign of intuition; the fifth Race was under the sign of the intellect) as announced by the Sun and the Stars, appears the Prophet who will go down in history as the proffered example. To be followed by great masses and requiems, man's expression of repentance and recognition. Christe Eleison! Think of this Great Initiate coming toward us on His way of the Cross, bringing all his love, knowledge and power, to harmonize the heart of the world and initiate it with the new Cosmic currents. An example. Think how much courage it takes to **want** (to do something); to be **capable** (of doing it); to **dare**; and to **do** it (willingly and in silence). How could he not remember those who had the same courage before him, the ones who were his models. On Mount Sinaï. On the Mount of Olives. On the black Cross of Golgotha. Christe Eleison! The Inquisition, the Pharisees, the Sadducees, the intelligentsia and the mass media! How could he not know history? The flight of Ram across Europe. The flight of Moses across the desert. The flight of Jesus at Christmas time. Will there be another flight? How could he not hear the terrible indictment: Krishna, Zoroaster, Orpheus, Socrates, Pythagoras, Jesus. Death! Imagine. Time repeats itself. If today you feel neither repentance nor recognition, it's because, once again, you have voted for death. Christe Eleison!


Well... at the approach of the year 2.000, there are thousands of us who do NOT wish the death of the Prophet, thousands of us who await his coming, who are preparing for his coming... he is our romanticism, our refuge, and our high fortress. Thousands of us are for the great spaces of the heart and the imagination, and I am sure that in the villages and in the cities, the provinces and the fields, there are millions of us with a taste for brotherhood, ready to breathe with him and march along with him and recognize each other as we do. Come, my brother, put your step in rhythm with his, it is time, the dawn is full of freshness and new beginnings, summer is here, the path is open, it is warm. Ahead of us, the Prophet magnifies the air with his powerful aura. He has left his garden and his vineyards, the fragrant rose-laurels. During the night, he read the ending; now, alone, he has climbed the hill to where the day is breaking. Come, I will lead you, my brother, up this path of freshness and new beginnings in the spaces of the heart and the imagination, to mingle your breath with his, your step in rhythm with his, your soul unfolding with his as he walks ahead of you on the path to the sunrise, bearing history. Come, you will not be alone, there are millions in the world moving toward the Spring for a drop of water, toward the Sun for reflected light, toward the Heavens for space amid the stars, toward the Heart for Love. Millions of us think of nothing else. It is our politics, our prayer, our choice, our faith, our battle. Come, there are grandiose things in store for this planet: signs don't lie. The sons of Herod are coming in view, Barabbas is going to be freed by those who want the Prophet to die. The seasons have come round full circle. We are not surprised, but if we could only seize hold, not of the Inquisition for once, but of the greatness, the grandiose circumstance, not the treachery of the heart, but the grandiose circumstance: Aquarius! Ganymede, holding in his arms a vase filled with solar water. Come, my brother, come and watch the Sun rise!

## THE GOLDEN AGE

An old parchment was discovered a few years ago in the South of France, inscribed with the following verse by Nostradamus, the great astrologer famed for his predictions («Centuries Astrologiques» – 1555):

«To a humble family will fair child be born
From a Balkan country will this Eagle fly
To dwell in the Land of the Coq
His name the same as mine the world will long recall
His voice the peoples of the earth will hear
And following upon upheaval and disaster
A New Age will begin.»

Maître Omraam Mikhaël Aïvanhov was born of humble parents in a Balkan country (that is history). Nostradamus calls the heralded Being an Eagle. «When man sublimates the energies of Scorpio he becomes an Eagle», say the Initiates. France (where the Master lives), is known as the land of the Coq. Visitors to the shrine of Nostradamus at Salon-de-Provence, in the Church of Saint-Rémy, have seen the name inscribed on his tomb: «Mikaelis de Nostradamus». And everyone will agree that the predicted upheavals have already begun. Maître Omraam Mikhaël Aïvanhov was born in 1900, at the beginning of the century in which Aquarius was to manifest itself in the shape of «upheavals», such as the first two World Wars. The third one is on its way... I say this not because I wish it, but to raise the question: who but the Initiates can stop the tide of violence?

Nostradamus was not the only one to prophesy the advent of the Prophet Mikhaël. There is a passage that refers to it in the Bible (the Book of the Prophet Daniel), and one in the Dead Sea Scrolls. C.W. Leadbeater of the Theosophical Society, and Rudolf Steiner, Founder of the Anthroposophical Society, also proclaimed Mikhaël as the coming Prophet. Here are a few lines from the book: «Who Is Maître Omraam Mikhaël Aïvanhov?»

«Leadbeater suddenly announced: «It will not be long before an extremely gifted Initiate, a Great Initiate, will bring the world a culture of the Sun, confounding everyone with his simplicity and profound knowledge.» Someone asked: «Do you mean Krishnamurti, your friend and disciple, supposed to be the reincarnation of Christ?» «No, no,» replied Leadbeater. «This person is from Thrace, the land of Orpheus.» «Do you know his name?» they asked. «Yes.» «Well, tell us, tell us!» «His name is Michael, or, in Hebrew, Mikhaël. You know that in the Kabbala it says that the Archangel Mikhaël is the protector of France. Mikhaël will appear in France.» «But when?». Leadbeater thought for a minute, and replied: «Before we reach a third of the century, but the height of his influence will not be felt until later on, toward the end of the century.»

«This was in 1906. Maître Omraam Mikhaël Aïvanhov arrived in France in 1937.

«Rudolf Steiner, during a lecture in 1924 at the Goetheanum in Switzerland, said the following: «All true thinkers are subordinate to Mikhaël, he is considered the Regent of Cosmic Thought. Mikhaël has freed thought from the bondage of the brain, opened up the way to the heart, and liberated the enthusiasm of the soul. To understand that is to welcome Mikhaël in our inner life. Thoughts that can grasp the spiritual emanate from the hearts that beat for Mikhaël, the flamboyant Lord of Cosmic Thought.»

«Steiner went on: «To be more concrete, one might say that Mikhaël, whose voice previously came from above, now is heard within ourselves. From now on we will receive him in our souls. The solar element that man has been receiving through the ages will shine in his soul and he will become conscious of an inner Sun. Not that he will feel any less alive during the time between his birth and death, but he will know for a fact that during his sojourn on earth his inner Self is guided by the Sun, he will have proof that he is illumined by an entity whose light dispels the darkness of his earthly existences, but only if he has acquired a certain knowledge.»

That Maître Omraam Mikhaël Aïvanhov should be the one to launch the new era from the beginning is not surprising to anyone who has watched him live over a period of more than thirty-five years. It is history. In his horoscope, he has the Sun and most of his other planets in the Constellation Aquarius, which is why he receives intimations of a new era long before other people, as mountain peaks are the first to receive the Sun's rays. All the grandeur of his past lives is revealed to him, for an event of such magnitude, a grandiose Cosmic Event, requires centuries of planning. The coming of Aquarius is the Cosmic Event, bearing the Living Water of the New Life to mankind.

To return to the Eagle and the Scorpion, Nostradamus being a great Astrologer, he knew that in the Initiatic tradition, the Scorpion replaced the Eagle in the group of Seraphim, the Holy Beasts of the Kabbala, the Hayoth Ha Kadosh, who sing «Holy, Holy, Holy, Lord God Almighty,» before the Throne of God. They are the Lion, the Calf, the Eagle, and Man. Since the Fall of Man, the Eagle has become a scorpion, symbol of sexual force. The Master has the power to transform fluids, because of his rising sign (Scorpio), as Astrologers will confirm. He can therefore transform man! He is the solar Mage of the New Life.

Therefore I write: the most important exercise the Master puts us through in his School is to realize the flowering, the New Life, so that brotherhood may flourish; I write this for all scholars, philosophers, and political leaders whose mission is brotherhood. Let them respond according to their hearts. They know now where their hearts can lead them and where their future lies. Let them accept (since their role is to be brotherly) the new policy of brotherliness. Let them grasp THIS Triple Programme (as they call it) and the three things that make it the heart and soul of the grandiose Cosmic Event:

The Lotus Pond

The Master and his Brother, Alexandre

The Master and a Child

1.   The Universal Solar Model, to be imitated by all scholars, philosophers, political leaders, artists, builders, parents and children of the New Era.

2.   Enlightenment, as to the two fluidic opposed and contradictory currents that spoil our lives and our love, and ruin our relationships because we don't know what their effect is... only the Initiates are initiated.

3.   Spiritual Alchemy, to transform our characters, so that men may meet each other on the high plane where love joins love, in the flowering.

Or in other words:

*   **A Universal Model** to etablish the heliocentric order without which Brotherhood will never come into existence.

*   **A Knowledge** of our two natures, one brotherly and one not, without which Brotherhood will not survive.

*   **A Transformation** of our primitive mammalian fluids, without which the Brotherhood of the Golden Age will never be.

That is the solar revolution created by Maître Omraam Mikhaël Aïvanhov, of which he is the living and majestic example. I am a witness. I say this for the people whose role and duty is to recognize reason, to be rational and fair, and who might therefore see to it that it is talked about in articles, papers and books, on platforms, before microphones and cameras, perhaps in song. And since to be fraternal is also part of their role and duty, they might announce that man will never be able to realize brotherhood until brotherhood is founded on the Sun, the only thing that can supply our infinite need for Light, Love and Life... and Liberty, the dream our revolutions are made of. Then everyone would want to practise that Liberty, they would think of nothing else.

May that happen soon.
For the time approaches.

Now we are there, at the height of the solar revolution. Mothers have borne the knights and geniuses they longed for; men are masters of their thinking, they know how to imagine their solar future, they control the etheric body of the earth (vegetation, atmosphere, climate, etc.). They assume their responsibility. The Golden Age is here! History advanced in the way we foresaw, the world went from the agricultural revolution to the industrial revolution, to the scientific revolution, to the solar revolution (the one having to do with the quality of life). The following words are by Maître Omraam Mikhaël Aïvanhov:

«As humans go further and further away from the light, everything becomes more and more complicated, until now the situation is practically inextricable. The moment we go away from the light, or transgress the law, or deviate from the path, things complicate themselves.

«Think of this image: it is summer, the Sun shines, the weather is warm, life is wonderful! Everything blooms: plants, flowers, birds, animals, human beings. There is plenty of opportunity to do all kinds of things. Winter arrives: heat, coal, oil, reserves to think about; bad weather makes it harder to communicate, in the fog and snow there are more accidents... you see how complicated everything becomes when light and heat are lacking?

«When man finally understands that he must forever move toward the Sun, toward light, toward God, everything will become clear, simple, and easy. Not all at once, perhaps, it will take years to put things right, but that is **the only way, the only method that will work.**

«Now, there is one thing lacking in the lives of human beings that is absolutely essential... a thing no scientist, philosopher, thinker, or clergyman ever mentions. It is this: everyone in the world learns, practically at birth, that they need three forms of nourishment, solid, liquid, and gaseous. But no one has ever told people that they must also nourish themselves with the fourth element called fire. It was the Alchemists who originally assigned this element to the realm of fire, making four elements: earth, water, air and fire; between them, they do everything that needs to be done on earth. If we nourish ourselves only with the first three, a whole element is lacking; not only that, the fourth element, fire, is the most important. No one has pointed out the fact that we can live for several days without eating, a day or two without drinking, and only a few minutes without breathing, but how long can we live without heat, without fire? Those who don't know will answer several years, but the truth is that you can't exist more than a minute without heat: the instant the heart grows cold, man dies. As long as his heart is still warm he can be revived, up to several days after his apparent death. That is why heat, or fire, is the most important of the four elements, why fire comes first for us, why we count most of all on the light and heat of the Sun's fire, especially at dawn... later on in the day, it is not the same. We nourish ourselves with fire as the Sun rises, like fruit we ripen under its rays. Fruit that is never exposed to the Sun is bitter, acid, tough, insipid, ugly... inedible.

«As below, so above», said Hermes Trismegistus.

«Instead of making fun of us and throwing mud and slander at us, it would be better if everyone did as we do, as the first man did: when Zarathustra asked Ahoura Mazda how the first man nourished himself, Ahoura Mazda answered: «He ate fire and he drank the light!»

Here, we discover that life unfolds in three stages, which helps us to understand the Cosmic Event. First comes the moment when the seed takes root; then the time for growth, the stem, the tendril, branches and foliage, then the blossom appears! Whereupon the flower fades and it all begins again. The Prophet appears in time for the new beginning, the new seed.

The time for meditation within, the time for expansion, the time for the flowering, and then the new beginning. It is true for flowers, for society, for civilizations, for the first grade as for the Initiatic School. Nothing can stop the Cosmic process, all life is subject to it, because people and things are subject to universal entropy (degradation of energy) and must continually be renewed by this trinity of light, heat, and life. It is what makes history. First the light and the seed it bears, then the spirit within, then the acquired knowledge, and then the Prophet come to launch civilizations in the name of Christ, the solar Spirit. The Master says: «Whoever wants to work with the Christ principle which is eternal and steadfast, that man belongs in the Great Universal White Brotherhood. He is never destructive, never against Christ, nor is he trying to bring in a new religion, no, he is simply refusing all the ancient, outworn forms now too limiting. Whoever wants to stay with the existing forms shows that he does not understand the principle, he is convinced that form will save him and goes on quietly sleeping, believing himself protected. Yes, form is stultifying. Those who don't rely on form but work with principles, evolve. It is written in the Gospels: «The letter killeth but the spirit giveth life.» Laziness is what makes people cling to the letter, to form. When their spiritual activity ceases, they replace it with form. That is why I am always urging you on toward the Spirit that gives life.»

Yes, this period of light and the Spirit is the beginning, very few know that it is history in the making: the time of the seed. We hear the Word, we listen! We have faith, we believe! We are in the dark, we think about light, like the first Christians hugging the shadows, tracing the sign of the Fish in the dust to identify themselves. Are we the first disciples of the Era of Aquarius, identifying ourselves as we search for water on the barren slopes of Mount Esterel? The time of the Spirit. The Initiate spoke the Word: we nourished ourselves with it; he gave us faith: we drank it in. It was the time of light and darkness, of the Initiate speaking the Word.

After this first period came the time of the Soul. Close upon the heels of the Spirit that emanates life, comes the Soul that fills it with light. The time of stalks and tendrils and branches and foliage. The time of communication, space, currents, meetings, words of love, great enthusiasm, tears of joy. We sing. Joy flows like sap in the vine at the thought that Paradise is at the end. The time of the warmth of the heart. We live it.

And then, no one knows how (things went so fast), the buds appeared and opened, and the flower appeared. The third period. The expression of the Life within. The seed stays in the ground a long dark time before the stalk comes up, all Fall, all Winter, part of the Spring. And then, all of a sudden, the flower is there. It blossoms! The beauty is astonishing. But even the flower must arrange for survival, energetically and chemically: the economy! It needs the sky, the light, water and food. Plans will have to be made to take care of the crowds that will come to see it, there will have to be roads, parking areas, dormitories, kitchens, bakeries and vegetable gardens, orchards, vineyards, organization. It is the time for economic realization, the time for dynamic and material things, for regulations and badges and administration, for civilizations as well as for Schools which are nothing but condensed civilizations. They live as the flowers do, in three periods, using for each period the people who are chosen for a particular role and time, who will disappear once the role is terminated. Three stages : the time for thinkers, the time for song, the time for bulldozers.

During the last period, the economy, something seems to happen, to the flower, it stops growing and begins to fade. It is to-day. The flowering over, gloom sets in, in the heart. The heart is no longer as strong as the economy. It tries to survive by strategy, it tries to revive hope. It claims that life is beautiful, but it is the effect of drugs and a long cry from the seed and the spirit. «Things are bound to change», we say. Nothing will change unless we begin again and go toward another flowering. It is precisely at the moment when everything seems to crumble and lose its original idealism, in Schools as in Society, that things are about to begin again. The grandiose Cosmic Event. The time of the Prophet. The time of the new beginning, the renewal. Extremely powerful planetary configurations  have long been forecast by scientists for some time in the 1980's, the earth will be rent apart by deep solar furrows, at which time, as St. John revealed in the Apocalypse, the stars will fall from the heavens, the petals from the flowers, and the Son of Aquarius will come upon us like lightning !


Lightning !
Take the three stages historically :


The Initiates came first with light, with understanding, with the seeds of wisdom that flowered into Love. But we weren't able to love.

Then they came with the warmth of love, and with great imagery in their hearts, with Christmas hymns. Jesus, an example of abnegation that has never been equalled, said the word Love. But we weren't able to love. And now we are at the fratricidal laser.

What will happen my brothers, if we don't do something? History continues, history repeats itself, history is logical: there was Light from Heaven, there was Love from Heaven, and now there will be Power from Heaven (thunder and lightning). Is it so that life will survive, so that the word Love will finally spring forth out of our wounds like living water? LOVE!

The Age of Aquarius is here.

The Time of the Prophet.

**«... And there shall be signs in the sun and in the moon and in the stars; and upon the earth distress of nations, with perplexity; the sea and the waves roaring; men's hearts failing them for fear, and for looking after those things which are coming on earth: for the powers of Heaven shall be shaken.**

**«And then shall they see the Son of man coming in a cloud with power and great glory.»**

**St. Luke 21 : 25**

N.B. This is the record. I have seen it. One day the reality will pass into legend. Then they will narrate the legend.

PRINTED IN FRANCE
DECEMBER 1979
PROSVETA EDITIONS, FREJUS

– Nº d'impression : 1160 –
Dépôt légal : 4ᵉ trimestre 1979
Printed in France